The Franchise MBA

Mastering the 4 Essential Steps to Owning a Franchise

By **NICK NEONAKIS, MBA**

Written with Aditya Rengaswamy and Sagar Rambhia

www.TheFranchiseMBA.com

RECOMMENDATIONS

"This is a powerful book. Whether you're in show business or the franchise business, the keys to success are the same; standing up for what you believe in, preparation, courage, persistence and excellence in your craft. Nick Neonakis delivers these keys with the Franchise MBA."

—Richard Belzer

Actor, Law & Order

Philanthropic Capitalist

"It's hard to believe that a book on the franchise business could be smart, definitive and -- brace yourself -- fun to read. But Nick Neonakis has pulled it off, because this one is. If you're even faintly considering a jump into the business, buying this book ought to be your first step. It's terrific."

—Tucker Carlson

Fox News

Co-Founder: The Daily Caller

"Nick Neonakis has written a skillfully crafted, comprehensive primer on franchises, a valuable 'must read' for anyone considering franchise ownership as a means to achieve personal wealth and the freedom associated with business ownership."

—Richard L. Osborne

Theodore M. Alfred Professor of Management

Weatherhead School of Management

Case Western Reserve University

"The Franchise MBA is an elegant treatise on franchising as a business strategy. Franchising accounts for 1 in 7 jobs in the USA, and as a distributed business model has endured through time, where businesses have passed from one generation to the next. Nick Neonakis demystifies the complexity of franchising and allows for a view into our world of creating value one franchise at a time"

—Charles E. Chase

President and CEO

FirstService Brands

"Do you want to make money? Do you want to feel the freedom of running your own business? Read this book—no, consume this book! Nick and his co-authors have de-coded the Rosetta Stone of small business."

—Distinguished University Professor Richard Boyatzis
Case Western Reserve University
Co-author with Dan Goleman and Annie McKee of the international best seller, Primal Leadership.

"The Franchise MBA is a book that transcends franchising and crosses into a solid understanding of how to evaluate your core abilities. I recommend this to any business leader or aspiring entrepreneur"

—Neil Patel
Publisher and CEO: The Daily Caller
Former Chief Policy Advisor to Vice President Cheney

"The decision to start your own business can be a daunting and intimidating task. The Franchise MBA lays out an excellent roadmap for those on their journey to independence. Nick Neonakis does a superb job of demystifying the process and provides the reader the tools needed to ask the right questions and make informed decisions."

—Robb King II
SR VP Franchise Development
Paul Davis Restoration, Inc.

"Becoming a business owner is a significant undertaking and you want to make sure to stack the deck in your favor. Nick and this masterfully written book will help you do exactly that. I would recommend Nick and The Franchise MBA to anyone seriously considering this exciting step into owning a franchise business."

—Andrew Horton
Chief Development Officer of the St. Gregory Development Group & Franchise Owner

"The Franchise MBA is a MUST READ if you're looking into any Franchise."

—Adam Ogden
CEO JuiceBlendz & YoBlendz
2012 " Entrepreneur of the Year"

"Buying a franchise is as much an emotional decision as a financial one and the Franchise MBA really offers a comprehensive review of how to evaluate both aspects of the decision making process. This is an excellent source for anyone considering a franchise and is written in an engaging, fast paced manner."

—Todd Leff

President and CEO

Hand and Stone Franchise Corp

"The Franchise MBA is a must read for anyone considering franchise ownership. Let Nick Neonakis become your "Franchise Sherpa" in the exploration of business ownership. Nick is a highly skilled and experienced guide who will provide a safe passage for you and yours. Take this exciting journey...you are likely to learn as much about yourself as you will about franchising."

—Peter Barkman

VP Franchise Development

CertaPro Painters

"If the thought of being your own boss has ever crossed your mind, this book will help you uncover the path to get there. Franchising can be an incredible vehicle to achieve your income, wealth and lifestyle goals and Nick Neonakis carefully lays out the steps to get there."

—Alex Roberts

President, Mr. Handyman International

"The Franchise MBA" is the perfect book for well-seasoned or beginner entrepreneurs. Nick Neonakis has written a self-guiding tour book for franchise ownership. If you're thinking of owning your own franchise opportunity this masterfully designed book must be in your library!"

—Tim Evankovich,

President/Founder

The Cleaning Authority

"Straightforward, practical and honest... This is the type of advice one would want from a parent and it's exactly what Nick Neonakis delivers to readers of The Franchise MBA. When considering significant investment in a franchise, an investment that may be close to one's life savings, why wouldn't the individual want straightforward, practical and honest advice? Well, Nick delivers just that and has written a must-read for anyone giving thought to buying a franchise making The Franchise MBA is as valuable as a Harvard MBA!"

—Paul Segreto, CFE

CEO – Franchise Foundry

"The Franchise MBA is a superbly crafted guide from a respected industry veteran. His insights into understanding yourself and what constitutes your ideal franchise business will help you as you begin your journey. Nick Neonakis has written a book that is meaningful, accurate, and a lively read!"
>—Kurt Landwehr
>Vice President, Franchise Development
>Regis Corporation

"Nick draws upon his lifetime of experience in creating this useful and instructive overview of franchising."
>—Lane Fisher
>Partner at Fisher Zucker LLC

"After thirty years in franchising and many books read, I feel The Franchise MBA was the easiest for a layman to understand. Great insight from a great person with integrity. A must read if you want to get into franchising."
>—Rhonda Sanderson | President
>Sanderson & Associates
>The ORIGINAL Franchise PR Firm

"The Franchise MBA by Nick Neonakis is a solid asset for those longing to understand the essential value of franchising and achieving the dream of ownership of a franchised business properly."
>—Doug Schadle
>CEO - Rhino 7 Franchise Development Corp.

"The complex chemistry of franchising is deconstructed in this book into a simple and concrete grounding that will allow the men and women who are looking to commit their entrepreneurial goals through buying a franchise to process with real consciousness the opportunity and meaning of their decision making. It will become an important book for many people."
>—Edward Leaman
>CEO Growers and Nomads

"The Franchise MBA is the must-read guide for the hopeful entrepreneur. Look no further because Nick Neonakis nails it with the Franchise MBA."
>—David Lewis, CFE
>Best Selling Author of The Emerging Leader: Eight Lessons for Life in Leadership
>Vice President of Franchising Express Employment Professionals

"The Franchise MBA truly captures the essence of how to find a great franchise opportunity – hard hitting factual analysis combined with a thorough explanation of the emotions and anxiety that can accompany the process. Fantastic take home value in every page!"
>—Jeff Elgin
>CEO Franchoice

"Nick Neonakis is one of the sharpest franchise development leaders that I have had the pleasure of working with. When he dispenses advice, I am all ears."
>—Dana Mead
>Director Kahala Franchising LLC

"By carefully guiding you all the way through the steps of an intelligent and rigorous franchise search, The Franchise MBA is the best resource available to someone considering franchise ownership. If you are exploring self-employment as a means to achieving your dreams, this book is simply a must!"
>—Michael Cassidy
>Director of Emerging Operations
>Floor Coverings International

"The Franchise MBA is a "must read" for all Franchise Professionals, Business Leaders and Entrepreneurs. Nick has communicated his knowledge and understanding of the industry in a clear and strategic manner."
>—Rocco Fiorentino, CFE
>President / CEO Benetrends Financial
>Board of Directors, International Franchise Assn.

"In The Franchise MBA, author Nick Neonakis offers the reader an invaluable and guided pathway through what might otherwise be considered a maze, when considering franchise ownership. Broken down into the most important but easy-to-read steps, the franchise buying process is highlighted against the kind of introspective questions any business owner should ask before making the decision to buy a franchise."
>—Rosemarie Hartnett, CFE
>President, Abrakadoodle

"Franchising's one of the best ways to go if you're going to start a business in the 21st Century, and Nick's one of the best people to help you get there. Nick's book will help you clearly understand franchising and how your lifetime of experiences has prepared you to begin this next chapter in your life through franchising. Start with the first chapter of Nick's book and keep reading!"

 —Bill Grody
 Founder/former Chairman & CEO America's Best Contacts & Eyeglasses

"Franchising remains a great way to go into business for yourself but not by yourself. Reading books like The Franchise MBA and consulting with legal counsel before investing is a prudent step for any franchise investor."

 —Steve Caldeira
 President and CEO, International Franchise Association

"Great franchise companies understand the value of passion, purpose, people and process. The Franchise MBA takes you on a journey through the realities of owning your own franchise from start-up to mature and illustrates the core values and principles that drive success for the franchisor and franchisee."

 —Steven Greenbaum
 CEO PostNet

"Finally, a book that brings the franchise opportunity, one of most powerful and successful business models in the world, to life in a straight-forward and useful way. Anyone considering franchise ownership will find value in The Franchise MBA. Neonakis draws on a successful and broad career to offer a thorough education and practical guide through the personal journey and business nuts and bolts of franchise ownership. More importantly, this is not an academic book; this is for those who aspire to build income, wealth and lifestyle through the franchise model. This is a book inspired by passion to help others and the knowledge to make it real and useful."

 —Dan Steward

President & CEO Pillar to Post"I've known and worked closely with Nick Neonakis for over 10 years in the franchising industry. Nick's sharp mind, intuitive nature, critical thought process and empathetic approach to working with others have made him invaluable to me in our endeavors together. Nick knows his stuff and is always up to the task!"

 —Tom Wood
 President and CEO
 Floor Coverings International

"If you're considering a franchise as an investment, there isn't another franchise business book in the industry that you should turn to. You will live and breathe the life of a franchise owner with the knowledge and savvy of a franchise veteran, page after page. You will thank Nick Neonakis for the education you receive. From the shadows of a cave near Mount Psiloritis (you have to read the book), to the classrooms of the PhD's in franchising, this is a franchise bible - and a must for the investor. Buy this book!"

    —Bob McQuillan

    VP, Franchise Development for Hand & Stone Massage and Facial Spa

    Entrepreneur & Multi-Unit Franchise Owner

"Great decisions are the result of good process, and "The Franchise MBA" walks the reader skillfully down the path to their ultimate success."

    —Jeff Dudan

    CEO and Founder AdvantaClean

Typeset by: Sagar Rambhia

Cover Art Work: Oscar Gresh

DEDICATION

To Stephanie — You are my muse
To My Family — You are my rock

To All Franchise Owners — You are the inspirations for the Future

CONTENTS

ACKNOWLEDGMENTS

This book sprang from the many conversations on business and franchising I have had with my wife, Stephanie, over the years. Her intellectual curiosity, encouragement and support have given me the ability to put pen to paper. This book simply would not exist if it was not for her.

I would like to also thank my writing partners Aditya Rengaswamy and Sagar Rambhia. Their intelligence, dedication and tireless effort brought this book from concept to reality.

This book is the culmination of a body of advice given to me by a lot of people whose names are not on the cover and made possible by the hundreds of franchise owners I have had the privilege of working with over the years. The courage these individuals, and every franchise owner have shown in making their decisions through their unflinching resolve to succeed are at the heart of everything that is good with small businesses in this country. This book is really a tribute to the franchise owners who wake up every morning with the resolve to continue their journey. It is through their efforts and determination that their business becomes successful, their employees are paid, families are fed and lives are made better. It is through their actions that our great nation lives up to the entrepreneurial premise that we are a land of achievers who can accomplish any goal.

Throughout the writing of this book, we have been surrounded by individuals who have generously and graciously donated their time and wisdom. They did this not for any accolades but because they had a genuine desire to share their wisdom in order to make someone else's journey achievable. This selflessness of spirit is humbling when one thinks that the contributors to this book will probably never meet any of the people who read it and never have a chance to see their contributions put in place by you, the reader. The reason these people donated so generously of their time is that they know what it is like to stand on the edge of the abyss and think about risking it all on an entrepreneurial venture. They remember the good times and the bad. They remember the joys and pains of their decisions. They have known great success and failure. They have persevered and created businesses and lives that are possible only in this country. They have reached out to share with you lessons that they learned the hard way to make the journey you are thinking of embarking upon a little easier.

There are not enough pages to thank all the people who have lent a hand and a shoulder to push this endeavor along to fruition. There are a few who have touched this book with their wisdom and have shown such a genuine desire to share. We are especially grateful to Richard Osborne the Theodore M. and Catherine C. Alfred Professor of Management at the Weatherhead School of Management at Case Western Reserve University. Gorilla – as he is known to generations of students – has been a mentor, confidant and friend. It was in his class that I first met my wife and, many years later, my co-authors on this book. His spirit of entrepreneurial honesty and intellectual curiosity has left a trail of friends that stretches across the world. This book would not be possible without him.

The Weatherhead School of Management is an extraordinary learning center and we would like to thank George Vairaktarakis, Ph.D, and Richard Boyatzis for their structural and academic insights.

Multiple franchise and business experts have graciously and generously shared their valuable time. We would like to thank Jeff Elgin, Rhonda Sanderson, Paul Segreto, Edward Leaman, John Georgadakis, Todd Leff, Doug Schadle, David Lewis, Steve Greenbaum, Lane Fisher, Jania Bailey, Steve Caldeira, Alex Roberts, Tim Evankovich, Art Husami, Geoff & Sherri Seiber, David Nilssen, Rocco Fiorentino, Kurt Landwehr, Dana Mead and Neil Patel for the vast amount of knowledge they enlightened us with.

INTRODUCTION

Dear Reader,

Congratulations! You are interested in owning a franchise, and we will be diving into that over the next seventeen chapters. But first, I wanted to congratulate both of us for making it this far. Think about our ancestors. Think about how lucky we both are, the statistical improbability that is life. We have made it across the millennia to the point in time that you are reading this book and contemplating ownership of a business. Think of the animals that our forebears outran so that they would not be eaten. Think of the plagues that did not kill them, of the wars that they did not die in. To be here right now is really a pretty marvelous achievement.

Doing something new is always going to have an element of fear and excitement along with that whiff of potential future success. You may have had some uneasy thoughts or sleepless nights going over the question "What if it does not work out and I fail?" Yet, I would say that the very fact that you are here right now shows that you are the embodiment of all of your ancestors' luck and good choices, and as you think about owning a franchise or going into business for yourself, I applaud you! You have quite a history of surviving! However, there are many out there who are not looking out for your survival. Be wary of who you deal with.

During World War II, General Eisenhower met with Marshal Zhukov. They hit it off right away and as the night went on they raised their glasses in numerous toasts. Maybe fighting the same enemy had something to do with it, or maybe they shared the respect for each other that often forms between two men who have both achieved a great deal. Maybe they liked the vodka. They talked strategy, tactics, and statistics. Eisenhower asked how Zhukov was able to achieve such low losses of tanks to mines during offensive campaigns. Easy, said Zhukov, I merely advance men across the battlefield before the tanks. They blow up the mines so that the tanks can advance safely behind them.

Perhaps you are wondering why I am starting a book on how to buy a franchise with a passage on military history. Perhaps you are feeling a bit repulsed at the low level of care that Zhukov had for human life. Eisenhower certainly did. Zhukov cared more for attaining his objective than for the individual welfare of his troops. They were expendable, and his goal was not. Of course, if Zhukov's troops tried to disobey, they would have surely been shot dead.

Perhaps you worked for someone like Zhukov. Perhaps you know what it is like to run in front of the tanks. There are lots of Zhukovs out there, whether in good times or bad. They seem to show themselves a bit more during bad times than good as they desperately try and achieve their objectives. As Warren Buffett famously put it, "It is when the tide goes out that you get to see who has been swimming with no shorts on."

I decided to start this book in this fashion because over the years I have come to know many franchise companies, the founders of them, the CEOs who run them, the staff who operates them, and the franchise owners who put their hearts and money into running their own business. The overwhelming vast majority of these people are marvelous. They are Eisenhowers. Let us call these franchisors "Zors." Like Zorro. They are good people. They look out for their friends.

However, like every field, there are some not-so-marvelous people out there. When I started working on this book, we talked about this kind of franchisor, and one of my cowriters, Aditya Rengaswamy, said "These people are like Czars." I liked that, and I thought it was apt. Let us call this type of franchisors "Czars." They are people who would prefer to reach their objective and view you as expendable. They would have you run in front of their tanks. This book is designed to help put you *in* a tank, give you the tools to make a reasoned decision, and to actively test whether or not the tank you are looking at is the right one. If you choose to own a franchise, that franchise has to be the tank that is going to protect and move you forward! Equally as important, we have to figure out if we even want to be on that team and if the campaign is the right one for you. If it is the wrong team or you are pursuing the wrong campaign, no tank in the world is going to protect you.

Let us learn how to distinguish between Zors and Czars. Czars never want you to know who they are until it is too late. Unfortunately, it is not a simple matter to identify them as they tend not to live in palaces filled with Fabergé eggs, but they do treat their franchisees like serfs. This book will give you the tools and optics to recognize Czars when you come across them. Remember, you can always get a job and be treated poorly. Why buy a franchise and have that be the case?

My Background

I was born in Greece and moved to Summit, New Jersey when I was a child. My mother is American, my father is Greek. They met in Greece while she was on vacation. They came to this country to provide a better life for their children. I have two sisters and a brother. My mother's family came from Ireland in the mid-1800s and settled in Northern NJ. My mother was a French teacher for many years. My father grew up on the island of Crete during World War II. His family lived in a cave in the shadow of Mount Psiloritis, the tallest mountain in Crete, during the winter of 1942. He is a survivor. When he came to the U.S., working in an office was not a realistic possibility, so he went into business for himself. He ran a taxi business and a house painting business. He was the driver and the

3

painter. Between my mother and father's hard work, they provided a solid foundation for their family. They bought a house and sent all four of their kids to college. Three of us have advanced degrees, and we all speak multiple languages. You really cannot help it when your dad speaks Greek, your mom speaks French, and everyone else around you speaks English. Education was important in our family. So was hard work. The American dream was something that you could achieve, not something that just happened. Generations of immigrants to this country believed that if you rolled up your sleeves and worked smart and hard, you would succeed. I believe, to my core, that it is exactly the same today.

My first entrepreneurial venture was during the gas crisis in the 1970s. Cars were lined up for miles waiting to fill up the tank. Before heading off to school, we would put donuts and coffee in our red Radio Flyer wagon and go knock on the windows of the cars to sell the driver's breakfast. I will never forget the look of gratitude as they handed over their change. Even better, I bought my first pocket knife with some of the money I made- a real Swiss Army knife. I have it to this day. The pride of financial independence left a mark on me. I have worked ever since—delivering newspapers, cutting grass, raking leaves, shoveling snow, working in restaurants, and all the other kinds of things kids do to make money. Every kid I knew did the same. We all worked. That seems to have changed over the past few decades. I have not had a kid come and knock on my door asking if they could cut the grass in a long time. Have you?

I attended Trinity College in Hartford, Connecticut and graduated with a degree in economics and classics. I worked every summer and winter break. One summer I was a garbage man in Short Hills, New Jersey in the morning and a waiter at the Office Restaurant in Summit at night. Of course there was always a shower in between one job to the next! After Trinity, I moved back to Greece, where I ran a jewelry business on the island of Santorini. I met amazing clients every day, learned how to run an organized business, managed employees, and had a ton of fun doing it. I worked for eight months of the year then travelled the world for four months each year. I had followed my heart doing something I wanted to do, and I have never regretted it. After three years, there came a day when I decided to come back to the U.S. and get into finance. It seemed like the right thing to do, and the tide was certainly rising during the late '90s. I worked with high-net-worth investors and small businesses helping them structure their portfolios. I worked in the World Trade Center. While I was not there when tragedy struck, I think about it every day.

I decided to get an MBA at the Weatherhead School of Management at Case Western Reserve University. In addition to meeting an amazingly talented group of students, as well as passionate faculty and staff, I met my future wife Stephanie while I was there. I knew she was the one the minute I laid eyes on her. She had a daughter, Megan, when she was very young. She raised Megan, worked, went to college, and got an MBA. Stephanie is as smart and tough as a woman can be. She is also a knockout. It was the best moment of my life when I asked her to marry me and she said "Yes!". Over the years, we have added to our family and have two wonderful sons, Max and Alex. We are lucky and blessed.

Upon graduation, I entered the world of franchising and spent the next decade working with one of the largest publicly traded providers of real estate-related services to the commercial, institutional, and residential markets in North America. With brands like Stained Glass Overlay, Floor Coverings International, California Closets, Paul Davis Restoration, Certa Pro-Painters, College Pro Painters, Pillar to Post Home Inspection, Handyman Connection, and Colliers International Real Estate, the company has a significant footprint.

I have worked on both the operations and brand development side of franchising. In the beginning of my career, I had the opportunity to work on the operations side of franchising, coaching and working with franchise owners to grow their business. This work included nuts-and-bolts tasks, such as scheduling, financials, hiring, marketing, and production. I still practice a lot of the lessons I learned from the hundreds of business owners I worked with to this day. I was fortunate to have mentors from the organization who put big opportunities in front of me and gave me the chance to travel the world developing and growing brands. That is what I spent the majority of my franchise career doing: leading and working with teams of people to sell franchises and develop the brands. I have held director and vice president positions in various brands and loved every minute of it.

However, there came a point where I was travelling a lot more than I was spending time at home. When I analyzed myself and took stock of my strengths and weaknesses and what I wanted to accomplish, I decided I could only achieve what I intended by working for myself. What I am best at and what I love doing is connecting with people, problem solving, creating opportunities, and offering pragmatic advice. It is not easy walking away from a career where you like the people you work with, like what the company does, are paid well, and see a great career path. I had sleepless nights thinking if this was the right step. If you contemplate owning a business, or have owned a business in the past, you know where I am coming from. I made the entrepreneurial decision and have never looked back. I have the privilege of spending my time helping others with their business issues and spending more time with my family, businesses, and investments. I have independence and control of my time. It is a good feeling.

I am fortunate that the many years of working at a senior level in franchising afforded me a wealth of contacts throughout the entire spectrum of franchise businesses in the U.S. and abroad. I have been humbled and blessed to cross paths, break bread, and gain wisdom from some of the brightest minds in franchising. Any wisdom I can impart is merely my retelling and making available advice and frameworks that others have provided to me. While I am a lifelong student, I feel the satisfaction of being an educator; I know that the pragmatic advice I am able to provide my clients helps them in their journey.

The Book

Everyone wants to be independent. Few achieve this. You are probably reading this book because you are not happy with your current situation or are looking to diversify your business through a strategic acquisition. Over the years I have had the privilege of working with thousands of high-net-worth individuals in a very intimate way. Whether it was analyzing their investment portfolios or discussing the prospects of partnering with one of the franchise brands I represented, I had the opportunity to learn quite a bit about wealth in this country. My clients shared with me their financial data; their tax history; their hopes, dreams, and fears for the future. There are lots of common threads successful people share. I have also crossed paths with people who have less. Very often, there were only a few decisions and choices that were made along the way that separated the two groups.

More often than not I was amazed by the low level of accumulated wealth that people had after spending a lifetime working as an employee. Most employees make their employers rich. Most employees pay more in taxes than they end up with in their retirement accounts. If you're going to work hard, why not have the fruits of your labor compound and benefit you family rather than others?

Therefore, the purpose of this book is to help you create wealth through using a franchise vehicle as a business investment. It is my aim to provide you with information, frameworks, and stories to help you make an informed decision about whether owning a franchise is the right step for you. This book is not meant to convince you to own a franchise or a business. It may or may not be the right step for you at this particular time or, candidly, ever. Regardless of the outcome, if we understand what we are looking at, it is a lot easier to make that clear eyed determination. This book will provide you with a lot of information. It is easy to get bogged down in the weeds sifting through data when you are trying to wrap your arms around something new. Venturing into the world of franchising is something new that involves a lot of money, something outside your professional comfort zone, and has the potential to create the life of your dreams or curse you to a life of abject unhappiness. I promise you there will be times when you get lost in data as you look at franchises.

Here is a visual to think about that we will come back to as we go through this journey of understanding franchising. Imagine you are on the bank of a stream and wish to get to the other side. There are four big stones across the stream. The stones look pretty solid and do not have a lot of slippery moss on them. How would you cross? Well, let us not run pell-mell across the stream. Let us keep one foot on the bank and test the first stone and see if it will give us solid footing. Once we know the first stone is solid, we can put both our feet on it and put one foot on the next stone to see if it is as solid as the first stone. Let us do the same on every other stone as we go across, and we should get to the other side—or know that this is not a good grouping of stones if they do not feel solid. If a stone doesn't feel solid, let us not risk putting our weight on the stone.

Investigating a franchise is very similar. The bank of the stream you are on is your current life. Owning a franchise is the other side of the bank, the life you want to shape. The book is organized into four main parts. Let us call them the stones that we are going to step on to cross the stream. We will refer to these periodically through the course of the book. The four stones are as follows:

1. Introspective Self
2. Understanding the Franchisor
3. Understanding the Franchisee
4. Legal and Financial Details

I propose we follow this sequence in investigating franchise ownership. As we go across our stream, let us keep our footing on what we know to be solid and true. As we test out the next rock, let us keep one foot on the current rock so that if that rock is not solidly anchored, we can feel the wiggle. Sometimes a rock that wiggles is very dangerous. Sometimes all it needs is a bit of tapping down to get bedded properly and become safe enough to cross. For our purposes, that tapping down is becoming more educated about that step in the process. If we are standing on a solid rock and we cannot get that next stone to feel comfortable—well for crying out loud, turn around and go back to the bank. We can always walk up the stream and look for another set of rocks. If we rush, we may fall in the water.

Genchi Genbutsu.

Buying a franchise is an investment. Like any other investment, its purpose is to achieve a desired outcome. However, there are few investments that you can actively influence the performance outcome in the same manner as you can with a franchise. You are going to take a very significant position in a franchise—you are going *to own* it—so you had better be able to influence its outcome. You are going to be tied at the hip to the franchisor, so we are going to make sure the franchisor is a good one before we partner with him or her. Here is where franchising can be so wonderful. If we structure an investigation properly, we can go and see for ourselves what is going on. Try doing that with a mutual fund! So raise your hand and say "Genchi Genbutsu!"

Genchi Genbutsu is the Japanese term for "the place," and in this case, "the place where it actually happens."

Taiichi Ohno, creator of the Toyota Production System, used to take new graduates to the assembly line and draw a chalk circle on the floor. The graduate would be told to stand in the circle and observe and write down what he saw. Ohno would leave, and when he returned, he would check the graduate's notes. If the graduate had not seen enough, he would be asked to keep observing. Ohno was trying to imprint upon his future engineers that the only way to truly understand what happens on the shop floor is to go there. It is here that value is added and here that waste can be observed.

For Toyota, because real value is created at the shop floor in manufacturing, this is where management personnel need to spend

9

their time. For us, real value is created in the franchise location, so that is where we need to go and see what is happening.

Genchi Genbutsu is therefore a key approach in problem solving. If the problem exists on the shop floor, then it needs to be understood and solved at the shop floor.

Toyota has over 325,000 employees and manufactures almost 9 million cars a year. Genchi Genbutsu has been credited with making Toyota the company it is today. I am going to propose that if this simple framework works for Toyota, we can make it work for us.

I love franchising because you can actively pressure test every step in the process. You can visit with the franchisor; you can look them in the eye, break bread with them. You can spend a day or two or a week with other franchise owners. You can mystery shop the franchises in your town or across you state. Do you like the service? Do you like the product? You can talk with customers and ask them what they think of the company. You can ask them how often they use the company and how they heard about it. You can see firsthand what this business is about and ask yourself the important questions: Are you going to love this? Are you going to be excited to get up in the morning? Do you have the opportunity to make the kind of money you need to make? Is this real?

I remember working with a particular client and looking at a number of companies. I was skeptical of the opportunity. He was enamored with it. We built a framework to actively test the business. One of the tests we devised was to sit outside of a few of the locations with a little clicker, like the kind you used to see at baseball games to count attendance. The goal of our framework was to see how many people were going in and out of the location, and how many people were looking in and walking away because of the line. It probably sounds like a good business if there was a line, but the reality was it was not. The throughput of the customers coupled with the average transaction size was not sufficient to cover the fixed costs. The physical size of the business could not accommodate the bursts of demand, and to increase the size of the business would inflate the fixed costs to such a degree that a downturn in demand would be painful. We were able to build enough of a business hypothesis to know that this was the wrong business to look at. It is tough to do that with other kinds of investments. We will absolutely practice Genchi Genbutsu with any franchise business we are serious about.

We are standing on the bank of that stream. The opposite bank does not seem very far. Let us put our foot on that first rock and see how it reacts!

Summary

Beware of the man who forces you to run in front of a tank.
Test the rocks in the stream before you commit
Genchi Genbutsu – go see it for yourself.

ROCK 1 – INTROSPECTIVE SELF

CHAPTER 1 - ANXIETY AND EQ

Mark stood among the shallow waters, looking at the greener pastures on the other side. The graying of his hair worried him—but he had little to care for at that moment. "Who am I?" he whispered to himself. "Why am I not on the other side of the brook?" Mark has gone through a variety of experiences in his life. He has defined himself by many personalities, his college degree from a great university, his well-paying job as the director of IT at a respected company, his social activities in his community. Yet, over the past few months, he felt something was missing. A lack of control over his destiny overwhelmed him.

Walking along the water, he noticed his reflection blurred from the flowing stream. At that moment he wondered where he could be one, two, ten years from now. What life can truly bring him should not be a mystery, should it? He hoped his reflection in the flowing water would clear with the passage of time. Yet time only seemed to further blur the little he could comprehend.

The greatest competitor you'll ever come up against is self-doubt.

—John McGrath

You want to know yourself better? A lot of people talk about "owning their own business," but they never translate these thoughts into actions.

To many, business ownership seems tough; this is the primary reason people avoid entrepreneurship. To effectively take your place as an owner of one of the twenty-seven million small businesses in America, you need to work proactively to be a success. Crossing the first rock of this book will help you answer the following three questions foundational to business ownership shared by Professor Richard Osborne, The Theodore M. Alfred Professor of Management at the Weatherhead School of Management and one of my significant mentors:

1. Does your professional background prepare you to run the business you are buying?
2. Is your family fully on board with your plans?
3. If you are buying an existing business, what is lost when the previous owner leaves the business? Do you have a plan to compensate for the loss of his or her skills and experience?

This section will empower you with tools to conquer your fears of owning a small business, and educate you on how to make the right decisions as a leader. While you may feel motivated to dive into entrepreneurship, you might suffer from one of the many symptoms of fear. You may have cold, sweaty hands, a racing heart, or butterflies in your stomach. This feeling grows as you spend more time dwelling on the thoughts that you are experiencing. I am here to teach you how to conquer this anxiety—with preparation. The negative thoughts fade as we prepare, and the fear we experience fades too. While in practice this is easier said than done, keeping focus on preparation can take the focus off of negative consequences. It is like parachuting; if you rush through all the equipment briefing, safety instructions, techniques, and training, you may get injured or die. With your small business, if you are focused and follow the steps outlined in this book, you will greatly increase your chances of success.

The standard metric of intelligence, Intelligence Quotient or IQ, reflects behaviors that demonstrate thinking and reasoning abilities. IQ does not account for managing intelligence during times of emotion. In fact, a lot of success has nothing to do with technical skill and IQ, but rather Emotional Intelligence (EI). EI is the ability to recognize and work with your own and others' emotions. Unlike IQ, emotional intelligence can be learned and developed.

There are many leaders, not just one. Leadership is distributed. It resides not solely in the individual at the top, but in every person at every level who, in one way or another, acts as a leader to a group of followers—wherever in the organization that person is, whether shop steward, team head, or CEO.

—*Primal Leadership* by Daniel Goleman, Richard Boyatzis and Annie McKee

Empathizing with and caring for others may be the difference between your small business succeeding or failing. There are five pillars to emotional intelligence: self-awareness, self-management, motivation, empathy, and social skills. The first step is simple: to relax. You have already taken the first step. By picking up this book, you will be presented with the tools to learn these five steps, which will give you a solid understanding of franchising. As you progress in business ownership, understanding emotional intelligence will help you deal with customers, venders, business associates, and employees.

1. Self-awareness:

    Self-awareness means knowing your feelings and using your intuition. It allows you to keep working towards your goals in the face of obstacles. Self-awareness goes together with social awareness. Knowing how others are feeling, how your customers and clients are doing without them telling you in words, can allow you to constantly adapt your business to be best suited for your market. Self-awareness relates directly to self-management, or making sure that you do not fall apart under stress.

Are you self-aware?
- Can you admit when you are wrong, and do you apologize when you are?
- Are you aware of other people's social cues?
- Do you ask others how they feel about situations?
- If you answered yes to these questions, you are most likely self-aware.

2. Self-management:

While you have learned to identify emotional influences through awareness, the next step is to control these influences and not allow them to command your decisions; managing your staff requires managing your emotions. Managing your emotions allows you to make good decisions and make valuable contributions at work. When faced with the emotional influence of negative feedback and criticism, you can take steps to control your anger and maintain composure.
- Can you manage your emotions?
- Do you get particularly emotional under stress?
- When your beliefs are challenged, do you feel the need to lash out?
- When you feel angry, do you allow this feeling to make your decisions for you?
- If you answered no to these questions, you are successful at managing your own emotions.

3. Motivation:

Starting a business requires two types of motivation: the motivation to initiate and the motivation to persevere. Both types of motivation require you to use your instinct to guide us to our goals. This allows you to strive to improve and continue in the face of setbacks. You as a business owner must be prepared—things will not always go as expected, but this is part of the journey.

- Do you have the motivation to start and run a business?
- Do you know what you really want?
- Are you willing to go out and seek, even discover, opportunities that align with what you want?
- Do you have a clear set of goals and ambitions that you will be willing to adapt to make a successful enterprise?
- If you answered yes to these questions, you have motivation.

4. Empathy:

Empathy is crucial in sales, and sales are the foundation for a new business. You want to build rapport to bring customers back. Empathy allows you to step outside of your own shoes and adopt the customer's perspective. Identifying emotional influences in others and empathizing with them can also prevent conflicts in the workplace. Ultimately, empathy allows you to communicate differently to diffuse anger and produce a productive environment.

- Do you pick up on other people's feelings?
- Can you pick up quickly if someone says one thing but means another?
- Do you find it easy to put yourself in somebody else's shoes?
- Can you quickly spot when someone in a group is feeling awkward or uncomfortable?
- If you answered yes to these questions, you have

the ability to empathize with others.

5. Social Skills:

Every small business owner should focus on developing lasting workplace relationships. There is little room for harsh leaders while leading a team. The stickler for the rules, the uncaring, and the aloof types of bosses can ruin the social dynamic of a company. People look to the business owner for leadership styles too. If there are tough leaders up the chain, it trickles down to everyone else and creates a hostile work environment. An emotionally intelligent leader fosters emotionally intelligent employees.

- Do you have skills to lead a team as one cohesive unit?
- Do you resolve disagreements in a non-confrontational manner?
- Do you listen to both sides of a story before making critical decisions about who to keep on your team?
- Can you quickly bring a group of people together and motivated under one idea?
- If you answered yes to these questions, you have the ability to lead a team.
- Why do we need these ideas as business owners?

Franchisors want star performers; they look for EQ – Emotional Quotient – which is defined as a person's adequacy in areas such as self-awareness, empathy and dealing sensitively with other people. They are looking for people who can motivate staff and maintain the integrity of their brand name. Franchisors want their franchisees to keep their locations open for a long time. You can be one of these star performers, and you are never too old to be a great leader.

IQ – Intelligence Quotient – is a measure of a person's intelligence as indicated by an intelligence test. IQ is stable through life, but EQ increases over decades, similar to maturity. Why not improve your EQ sooner and start your journey into entrepreneurship with a solid foundation? Do not lose sight of the fact that your employees are people, people with emotions that impact how they think and act.

While you can accelerate how quickly you develop EQ, age and experience are helpful when trying to start a business. Many are skeptical whether those in their fifties, sixties, and even seventies, have the ability start and run a new business. However, as you get older, you have more clarity about what you want because you have experienced many things in life; you have a greater understanding of what brings you happiness. This does not necessarily result in a myopic view of solutions based on a specified set of experiences; you can create an experience with accumulated wisdom to fill unsatisfied desires. The 2011 Kauffman Index of Entrepreneurial Activity found that Americans in their fifties and sixties created more firms than any other age demographic. Success is not guaranteed, but if you are enthusiastic about your product or service, ready to put in the hours, and surround yourself with a strong support network, you are prepared to be an entrepreneur.

How does EQ relate to success?

EQ is indirectly related to success predominately through modification of the fear of failure—an irrational thought that we will not succeed. It leads to procrastination and hesitancy as we constantly second-guess our decisions. Fear of failure is most harmful when it stops us from doing the things that allow us to move forward with achieving our goals. It interferes with motivation. Just the need to succeed can lead to paralysis by analysis as you predict a traumatic event from happening even without any reasons. Failure is simply a matter of perspective.

It is impossible for us as humans to go through life without experiencing failures. The challenge is not to face risk focusing solely on failure. This can create a quagmire of inaction. Failure can manifest itself in one of two ways: either we see it as the end of the world and a sign that we should not continue, or we can see failures as learning experiences, whether they happen once in a while, or on a daily basis. If we learn from failures, we are able to grow and keep from making the same mistakes again.

Your first loss is your best loss. Most people can't accept the first mistakes. As you grow, you'll make some good decisions and some not so good decisions. People who make the same mistakes will continue to do so until they're out of business.

—Steve Greenbaum, CEO of PostNet

Why do we need these ideas in the workplace?

How you feel about a restaurant is how you feel about its employees. When a customer interacts with a representative of a company, he or she can either feel better or worse after the experience; the experience then reflects on the company itself. Individuals who come from the old school philosophy of rule by intimidation are much less likely to create a sustainable environment where empowered employees go out of their way to help the customer.

Emotional Intelligence in the Workplace

Attitude:

An employee comes into the office looking a little worn down, not ideal for someone who is approaching customers all day. Rather than criticizing him with the words, "You do not look so good today," it is better for an employer to say, "Are you having a bad day? We all have those. What can I do to help? Why are you frowning?" By providing comfort to your employees, you are supportive of their emotions without being hurtful. This probably sounds like a no-brainer; just think of how much better our experiences would be in schools, businesses, and workplaces if everyone utilized EI.

Productivity:

A business manager who finds the pace of his subordinate's work unacceptable could say, "I could finish that job in half the time." This demoralizes and places a low value on the subordinate. Rather than criticizing, the manager can encourage the subordinate by saying, "Back when I was in your shoes as the new guy, it was a tough job for me too. Want me to show you how I did it?" This shows the acceptance of the supervisor and encourages the subordinate to excel at his job.

Values:

At the pillar of any business, from mom-and-pop shops to franchise giants, there are a set of core values and a clear vision. As a franchise owner, it is important to impart these values to your staff. Say a sales person comes into work and says, "I refuse to sell to this set of people because of the values of my culture and family." Similarly, if he was taught to discriminate against a set of people, he will continue to do so even as an adult. Encouraging an employee to adopt different values teaches supportiveness without fear of punishment. Emotional intelligence allows you to do this.

The Drive to Succeed

There are many great people in history who have experienced failure in their lives. A few prime examples are Thomas Edison, Steve Jobs, Bill Gates, and Richard Branson. Individuals like these have dropped out of college, and have been fired from places they loved working at. No one likes to fail. However, if you have not experienced failures then it is likely you haven't experienced great successes. Failure can be a transformational force for betterment. With 1,093 patents in his lifetime, Edison certainly knew success and how to get results. When asked he said "I have gotten a lot of results!

I know several thousand things that won't work!"

One of the key reasons people buy a franchise is to purchase the lessons derived from mistakes that someone has already made and paid for. In a successful franchise system, these expensive lessons have been learned and remedied and the proper way to operate has been spelled out. This testing of the business model is one of the reasons franchising has been so successful. Of course, there are failures in franchising and it's easy for our psyche to play games with us and make us think that maybe we'll fail too. If you let the fear of failure stop you, you will miss countless opportunities. To overcome fear, use the following four steps:

1. Analyze all potential outcomes
2. Learn to think more positively
3. Look at the worst-case scenario
4. Have a contingency plan based on the outcome of step 3

Setting goals and maintaining vision can also transform your fear of failure into the drive to succeed. If you are driving a racecar, or in your case running a small business, it is important to drive through the turn rather than driving into the turn. By driving through the turn, you accept that bad things may happen, and you do not let it affect your current performance and your chances of success. Fear only affects how you look at situations. It makes you less aware of the possible solutions and outcomes at that time.

What are your choices when someone puts a gun to your head?

What are you talking about? You do what they say or they shoot you.

Wrong. You take the gun, or you pull out a bigger one. Or, you call their bluff. Or, you do any one of a hundred and forty six other things.

—*Suits*

Summary

Be focused. Focus and preparation can transform fear to work for and motivate you. Gone are the old-school ways of academic intelligence in the workplace; emotional intelligence is becoming increasingly important to create star businesses and star performers. By adopting the five pillars of emotional intelligence—self-awareness, self-control, motivation, empathy, and social skills—you will have the tools to survive no matter where you work. Over time, and especially as a small-business owner, emotional intelligence can foster a healthy work environment.

CHAPTER 2 - FINDING YOUR WHY

Mark heard a noise coming from behind him. "Daddy! I am home from school," a small girl cheered. Turning around, he saw the joyous face of his youngest daughter. He had two other kids who were grown and out of the house, even though he helped support them as they got their careers started. Running, he embraced her and threw her onto his shoulder. They made their way back to his comfortable home.

Immediately upon entrance, his wife chided him for being so careless. "I do not want you to break your back, Mark!" she says. "The last thing we need is another medical bill! Clean those dirty feet of yours!"

Slowly, he put his daughter off his shoulders. Ignoring his wife's direction to tidy up, he made his way to his living room. He saw his father-in-law, Tom, watching some old movies from 1950s. Tom had been living with them for the past several months, and even though he cared for him, Mark sometimes longed for the days when they had the house to themselves.

Suddenly, he had a flashback to a weekend many months ago...

He heard his phone ring. It was his boss. "Strange, my boss never calls me on weekends," he thought to himself.

"Hello, sir. How are you today?" Mark answered.

"I'm okay, Mark. We need to talk first thing in the morning when you come to work tomorrow. I've had the office secretary clear up your schedule."

"What is this regarding?"

"I'll talk to you tomorrow." His boss hung up.

That day flew by as hordes of butterflies fluttered in his stomach. He had known this day was coming for a while. He had been through a few rounds of layoffs and had seen his old friends leave. New fresh faces replaced them. New fresh faces getting paid a third of what he was getting paid. New fresh faces who did not have family. New fresh faces who did not have insurance needs like he did. He knew what was about to happen.

The next day, Mark wore his finest suit and made his way to work. Upon entering the facility, he noticed the secretary acting strangely around him.

"Good Morning, Gloria," Mark said.

"Hi Mark. Tim is waiting for you," she replied nervously.

Mark got fired that day. His boss didn't call it being fired. He had a bunch of other things he called it. Something about a headcount reduction due to demand, and the division was being reorganized, and there was a new mandate from the CEO. The political correctness of it was mind numbing. Mark knew that the real reason was that he was an expensive guy, and the company was outsourcing a portion of his work and then filling the rest of it with younger, cheaper employees.

On the way out the door, his boss told him that he would have COBRA insurance for a few months and that he was at a great point in his career to look for new opportunities.

Mark wanted to punch him in the face. He had worked hard for his company. He had missed kids' birthdays; he had missed plays and soccer games. He had travelled to meet clients. He had worked on weekends. He had sacrificed for the company, and this is what he got in return. The shock was almost too much to bear... His heart flooded with disappointment. What would he tell his wife? His kids? So much of his identity had been tied up in his work. What would he do now?

Most of us are afraid to dig deep into understanding who we are. We feel comfortable with the surface self, coming back to the status quo again and again. Those that do things for material reasons rarely feel satisfied. Sometimes, even those that have deeper reasons for what they do feel proud, but not satisfied. A number of experts who have written about this topic, such as Simon Simanek, describe this journey through three basic questions. What? How? Why?

What am I doing as I live?

You need to understand exactly what you are doing. This extends to specific things like the type of job you have and the types you friends you spend time with. Tangible ideas and observable traits come into play to understand what you are doing. Questions to consider include:

- Where do you work to make an income?
- What activities do you engage in outside of work?

Itasca Community Library
itascalibrary.org
630-773-1699

Title: Franchise management / by
Michael H. Seid, CFE, a
Author: Seid, Michael,
Item ID: 31529002105121
Date due: 5/4/2019,23:59

Title: Franchising for dummies
Author: Seid, Michael.
Item ID: 31132009872098
Date due: 5/4/2019,23:59

Title: ILL Franchise MBA
Author: Neonakis, Nick
Item ID: 30131001717203
Date due: 4/16/2019,23:59

Planning a trip?
Get your passport here!
We're a passport acceptance
site.

How am I doing it?

How you are doing it refers to the path you are on to achieve your *what*. This could mean finding the right employer or choosing to be self-employed. It could lead to decisions such as going to college, or attending certain conferences. No matter what is desired, the path to obtain that *what* is important. Questions to consider include:

- Did you go through college to be able to do your job? What college did you attend?
- What training have you acquired to be able to do your job?
- Who have you chosen to associate with to increase the chance of success in your work? Do you spend time with your boss or other key players outside of work?

Why am I doing it?

The "why" part is the most difficult to answer, but it is by far the most important. This is the reason that you live. These are the things you would happily do if you were forced to wake up at three in the morning to achieve some end. This could range from growing and supporting a family to creating a legacy based on what you love. These are the underlying goals that shape who you are and create a sense of fulfillment when pursued.

Questions to consider include:

- When is the last time you felt excited to do something, and woke up early in the morning to do it? Why were you excited?
- What would you be willing to do if someone woke you up at three in the morning?
- What activities or people put the biggest smile on your face? What aspects of these things make your experience so enjoyable?

Most individuals prefer to focus on "what" and "how." Some individual may want to be an accountant when he or she grows up; therefore, he or she pursues an education to obtain a CPA certification. We are taught in collegiate and even work environments that this is normal. We are encouraged to think this way.

In fact, many businesses sell you their ideas the wrong way. They talk about what they do, and then show you how they do it. Finally, they ask you to buy it. This technique is not inherently flawed, but the greatest leaders of history and some of the more successful companies in our time completely flip this procedure. Figures like George Washington, Martin Luther King, and companies like Google have embraced this idea of "why" throughout their lives.

George Washington was not well equipped as a revolutionary leader. His forces were tiny compared to those of the British. His "what" or his army and resources that he worked with were limited in scope. His "how" was a bit more interesting and clever. He had a good sense of battle strategy. He knew he needed to find allies from all over the vast colonies, and foreign allies like the French. Through the forge of various tactics and people, he gave his weaker conglomeration of states a fighting chance against the most powerful army in the world, the British.

Now, his "why" is where he had the true advantage: Freedom from foreign rule, a desire to self-govern— all of these factors forged his spirit and his personality. The soldiers he recruited were not fighting like mercenaries protecting a nation; rather, they were fighting for their homes, for their family's freedom, for their children's security and they gave their blood and tears to fight for the chance to self-govern and be free. That belief in a nation defines this "why" —Washington's ability to grab his countrymen's innermost minds made him great.

Others joined Washington not as warriors looking for the ideal pay, but as warriors of conscience. They saw value in his beliefs, and joined him in the creation of one of the most enduring democracies in world history.

Martin Luther King is another figure who created this same sense of deeper purpose. His "what" was simple: civil rights. At a time when racial divides ran even deeper than they do today, he became a voice and a leader.

Dr. King's "how" was clearly defined—he ran demonstrations, organized committees, and gave speeches. However, all of these things did not set him apart. Other civil rights leaders at the time were doing these things as well. There were great orators in many states and leaders who fought for this cause through other means.

What set him apart was his "why." His "why" was a dream—a dream of a world in which all of his children could play with children of any race. His "why" was a belief that violence was not the way to achieve such higher morals. He wanted his beliefs to be based off of the freedom to live as he chose. He wanted to be accepted by any crowd and have an opportunity to find his calling. This message resonates with the thousands that attended the March On Washington, where over 25 percent of the attendees were not people of color. His message was a desire for the acceptance of every man, which he articulated before delivering the "what" and "how" of his strategy.

Franchisors develop their own dreams and ambitions. They are looking for franchisees to join them on a journey where their businesses revolutionize and standardize an industry in various locales. Choosing to join them requires an understanding of one's own dreams.

- What are your dreams and passions?
- What are you looking to achieve and get out of life?

Google follows this approach in their marketing and company images. Google is looking to show very innovative products not through its features, but through its purpose. They make products that challenge the current market offerings. They want to revolutionize how we interact with information and people through the Web. Their Web site even offers a "What We Believe" section that dives into the tenets of their goals and values. Google does not advertise a product; instead, Google advertises a lifestyle. That ability to advertise a lifestyle is what attracts investors and consumers alike.

All of these figures and companies can seem intimidating, and creating deeper visions is one of the most difficult things that anyone can do. Taking a moment to reflect and define these values is important. Some aspects of life that many value include family, time, happiness, and wealth; this is their "why."

Family

As shared by Maslow's hierarchy of needs, inherent in all of us is a desire to be supported and loved by a family. The implications of this desire are numerous and obvious. In fact, you are likely reading this book to make your family's lives better.

There is an interconnectedness among members that bonds the family, much like mountain climbers who rope themselves together when climbing a mountain, so that if someone should slip or need support, he's held up by the others until he regains his footing.

—Dr. Phil McGraw, *Family First*

Money

All families need a money stream to sustain them. You do not want to be living paycheck to paycheck, and having savings for unexpected events is crucial. Everyone wants enough money to live in a home, eat comfortably, and spend quality family time bonding with each other. If a family includes children, further implications can arise.

- Do you value family?
- Is creating wealth for your kin important just for your immediate relatives, or do you strive to create legacy investments that provide wealth for generations to come? Is

your business going to be the planting of a financial orchard? An investment that bears fruit year after year?

Time

A family will require time commitment. Unless family members are comfortable living very separate lives, with little interaction, there is usually a desire to do things together. This means that work cannot completely consume you. You need to balance your life.

- How do you wish to spend time with the ones you love?
- Children and grandkids can grow up fast—how flexible do you want your time to be?

Happiness

This value stems from an innate desire, but many times there are individuals who want more enjoyment in their lives. There are others who are willing to do things they do not enjoy to achieve a different end, but there are many who believe that doing things that make you happy will allow you to never work a day in your life.

From frustration to happiness- that is the greatest achievement.

—Tim Evankovich, CEO of The Cleaning Authority

A job or an activity that one is involved in needs to satisfy, provide time and money to pursue your interests. Realizing that no matter how fleeting time may seem, a positive attitude and determination creates happiness. Ask yourself: Where does your happiness stem from?

Achieving your Why

Being the Employee:

Being an employee is the most common way people earn an income. For many generations, this vehicle tended to be predictable in its scope and rewards. Being an employee used to result in a more certain income, and time available to pursue interests outside of work. Over the years, this stability has been brought into question. Long gone are the days when someone could work for one company, get a gold watch at their retirement party, retire in their sixties, pull in retirement benefits, and live in Florida. Average employees in this century have almost eight jobs before they retire.

The employment concept rarely builds a massive wealth portfolio either; however, a very small percentage can make it to the top of the business ladder. Those who are employees may not advance as fast as they wish to, and their financial desires may not be met. A common refrain from employees is that they have created massive gains for their company, and very little of that was shared with them. Add to this that you may not like your boss, who has considerable influence over the quality of your life. The Greek word for work is 'doulia' (δουλια) and the word for slave is 'doulos' (δουλοσ) or "he who is made to work". Many employees feel this way today.

Starting a Business—Start-Up Style

This form of starting a business is all about developing a new idea or concept. It can involve taking an existing concept, modifying it, and presenting it as a novel solution or service. The certainty of this income varies on many degrees, and some ventures are much more successful than others. These kinds of businesses have a reputation of consuming one's life. While start-up businesses do take up a significant amount of time in the beginning of the enterprise, as the enterprise matures, the time commitment to running a new businesses may go down. Job satisfaction tends to be higher, especially when the business you create aligns with your interests.

The downside of this approach is the unpredictability. No matter how much effort you put in, there is no guaranteed paycheck; however, with the right networks, products, financial planning, and customers, this kind of business model can achieve wealth while maintaining your values. Nonetheless, the failure rate of these types of businesses is the highest in any category.

Combining Different Vehicles

This is the most common approach to wealth creation. There are those who have a job and invest in markets. There are some entrepreneurs who own franchises and self-started businesses. One of the most effective methods to life success is to combine multiple vehicles to create satisfaction. None of these vehicles is necessarily wrong, but understanding your underlying goals can help determine which vehicle makes practical sense. Many franchisors will help you combine different vehicles by allowing you to run a franchise and investments, or work at a company and keep their franchised unit running on the side.

The Journey of "Why"

It is all up to you. Do not be afraid to probe deeper, and think harder about who you are. Do not be afraid to take time to ask others what they see in your personality and your values. Take time to write out what you do and how you do it. Writing is a powerful tool to help you understand and self-visualize. You do not need to necessarily write a journal, but take time to write out what inspires you. You have nothing to lose by doing this, and writing is an effective way to begin the journey of satisfying "why."

- Why do you live on this earth?
- What is your ultimate purpose?
- If I am the culmination of thousands of my ancestor's lives, what is my purpose to keep that chain intact for future generations?

These are all queries your journey of "why" will answer. Enjoy this journey, as it lasts a lifetime. Do not forget to keep coming back to "why."

If later in your life you feel like you are satisfying "why" —great! What now? How do I know if I am hitting my milestones and achieving what I desire? Binders! Take some time to create binders, computerized or paper, that are filled with moments from your "why." Whether it is a statement of equity that shows your holdings, or photos from your family vacations, every little piece counts. These binders should hold indicators of progress as well, not just the end goal. If you want financial freedom, having wealth to support your later life is something to celebrate and document.

Looking back in time is more than a mere perk of living. Smiling through pleasant memories is not just for joy. With it, we see much deeper images of the path we as men take.

—Anonymous

Down the road, this documented journey of what the "why" is and how you achieve it will not only inspire you to keep on going, but it may even end up inspiring others. The heroes of history that follow their "why" have always made it a point to leave some trail for others to follow—whether it was done through the media of the times or their own writings, it is a common thread these heroes all share. Figures such as Anne Frank, Lewis and Clark, Franz Kafka, and Benjamin Franklin have all written diaries that documented their lives. These works have served as inspiration to themselves and many others over the years. Why not start documenting your journey today?

Summary

Your life consists of three key components: your "what", your "how", and your "why". Realize that what you do and how you do it are the smallest aspects of your core. It is why you move that matters most. Taking time to figure out your why and acting to achieve these "whys" is crucial. Whether you own a business, invest in companies, or work for a company, seeing how these entities work together to satisfy and provide for your "why" is important.

Finally, do not forget to document all stages of the journey that satisfy your "why." Not only is it a great way to gauge progress and look back at your growing sense of accomplishment, but it could also end up inspiring future generations.

With a passionate pursuit of values comes a never-ending legacy.

CHAPTER 3 - ENTREPRENEURIAL ATTRIBUTES

Rolling around his bed that night, Mark knew that what truly mattered to him was his family. He had to let them know what was going on first thing in the morning, and he had to find work to provide for them. He was still years from retirement, and though his wife had a job as a teacher, they wouldn't be able to support themselves only on her salary. He looked into the future and wondered if he would end up like Tom, his step-father who spent most of his days watching television.

The next several months were difficult. His wife cried over trivial things, and his home life was filled with awkward glances and early goodbyes. His work had provided him with an outplacement service, and he spent time working on his resume and networking. He applied for hundreds of jobs. Sometimes he would have an interview. He even changed his resume so he wouldn't seem quite so old. The professional accomplishments that had once given him pride now seemed to hold him back as overqualified. He didn't have any meaningful offers of employment. If he wanted a job making one third of what he had made, he could find plenty of jobs. The people he interviewed with were years younger than him, and he often wondered if they didn't hire him because they were intimidated by his experience.

He started to feel that friends who had jobs were avoiding him, and people he had helped over the years didn't return calls. He had thought he had a great social network, but as time went by, he found that people who had called themselves his friend were actually mere acquaintances.

The whole world seemed against him, and as time went on, his daughter intuitively began to ask a lot of crushing questions.

"What's wrong, Daddy? Why are you sad?" she asked.

"Mommy, why is Daddy always in his office?"

Such words filled his heart with a deepening sorrow, and yet there wasn't much he could do to remedy the problem.

One day as he entered the outplacement office, his friend Jill pulled him aside. Jill had an upbeat look on her face as she pulled out a business card and gave Mark a huge smile.

"I talked with a new tech firm called Marina Technology, located in Green Lake Park. They are looking for an entrepreneurial-spirited man to be their Executive Director of Information Technology. I put your name in for that position. Here is the CEO's business card. I'm hoping you receive this post!"

This sounded like an amazing opportunity to consider, but Mark had little to no experience in an entrepreneurial venture. Most of his experiences had involved managing people and software applications. Could he even succeed in a post like this?

An entrepreneur is someone who uses other people's ideas, money, and time to create value. If you are like most people, you have never owned a business. How do you know if you are going about it the right way? The United States has always been a land of entrepreneurial opportunity, and we celebrate success in entrepreneurial ventures unlike any other country. Horatio Alger was one of America's earliest chroniclers of rags-to-riches stories and the legions of children he inspired. In Alger's first story "Ragged Dick", the protagonist goes from a street urchin who smokes, drinks and sleeps on the sidewalk to the respectable businessman, Richard Hunter, Esq through doing good deeds, being honest, frugal and working hard. You can succeed in this country if just work hard and do the right thing. These are simple themes from a simpler time but ones that hold enduring value and that shaped the American attitude towards business and upward mobility. That was true in the gilded age and, I believe, is true today. Winston Churchill encapsulated this when he said *"Broadly speaking, the short words are the best and the old words best of all"*.

There is no magic formula or perfect technique that leads to being an effective entrepreneur; there is not a particular way of acting that guarantees success. Yet, there are certain tactical behaviors that entrepreneurs share, and beyond these behaviors, their greatest success comes from their emotional intelligence and ability to implement various leadership styles. This chapter analyzes the behaviors that many entrepreneurs share and discusses the leadership styles that effective leaders of companies possess.

The Art of Doing Less

Work smarter, not harder.

—*Scrooge McDuck*

The most effective entrepreneurs know their strengths, find people to manage their weaknesses, and do precisely what is required for the company to succeed. They do not overthink things, and in the case of the franchise model, they do not spend too much time analyzing every small detail. Your goal is to lead the company, not ensure that product number two has the right shade of red. Franchisors sell you a business model for a reason, and you should follow it. Imagine being a business owner that not only needs to make a product, but also market it, account for it, and sell it to customers. You would have too many activities competing for your attention to effectively achieve the most important goal of running a cash flow positive business. This is one of the key reasons franchised businesses, as a whole, are more successful through start up than an independent entrepreneurial endeavor.

Embrace Accidents

Some things will go wrong when you start a new venture, franchise, or other project. The question becomes how to deal with it. The most effective entrepreneurs embrace mistakes and persevere through them. Some of them even create situations where collisions are forced to occur. They create an office space that forces interactions between various members of their staff. The chance of an interaction among employees being meaningful may be one in a thousand, but if you increase the interactions, chances are higher that something of meaning comes out. Entrepreneurs are never afraid of conflict or mistakes and embrace the idea of shared failures.

Imagine the crushing feeling of not hitting your sales target your first month owning a company. Do you just give up, and forget the business altogether? There is no way an entity can be perfect—and that is important to understand. The best entrepreneurs look at what went wrong and then how to address the deficiency for the next month's activities.

Let Others Lead

Leadership and ventures are a team sport. Similar to doing less, you must have the ability to give up your position of power when appropriate. If you fall sick one day, your company cannot fall to ruins. If others are not trained to understand your business with a passion to make something happen, it will not make sense to keep a business going long term. Unpredictability of life is reduced when entrepreneurs spread the risk.

Imagine the comfort you will have when you take a day off and know that a manager or a trusted employee is handling everything. He or she is ensuring the company is meetings its obligations for that day, and the work environment continues to create value. This is creating an orchard through a business.

I'm going to say the way to lead is from the rear, building leaders in the organization— provide people with the motivation with the tools, the motivation to succeed.

—Steve Greenbaum, CEO of PostNet

You Are *Not* a Risk Taker

One common misconception of entrepreneurs is that they are risk takers. This is far from the truth. They are risk calculators. Their decisions are based off of profit potential, planning, and hard work. Risk takers are usually gamblers, where one could strike it rich, but no planning or preparations is done. Running a company as a gambler will most certainly result in ruin. Oftentimes, when I speak with people who are passively looking at owning a business, they will often say one business or another " seems very risky". Over the years, I have come to believe that when someone says "this is very risky", without any reasoning or analysis to substantiate their claim, and then points to the general environment of owning a business as "risky" it is usually because they are mentally too lazy to perform an analysis of the business. Calculating risk in a business undertaking is a significant mental activity. It is hard. However, nothing worthwhile in life is ever easy, it?

The franchise model is designed to specifically make risk easier to calculate. There are three primary reasons why.

1. Franchisors have already built businesses and models that they have successfully run. These business models are made available to you. Knowing what you are doing lowers risk.
2. You get an FDD or a disclosure document that will give you a wealth of information about the franchise you are considering.
3. You receive training, support, and some sort of exclusivity, be it a region or a customer base.

These factors are significant. Mark Spriggs, associate professor and chairman of the entrepreneurship department at the University of St. Thomas' Opus College of Business, said the chance of success is "vastly greater" with a franchise than with an independent business. Roughly 80 percent of franchises survive five years in business, he said, while only 20 percent of independents are around that long.

"People will argue over the percentages, but it's two to three times more likely to succeed than the independent businesses," said Spriggs.

Emphasize Steady Progress

Most successful entrepreneurial ventures grow slowly and steadily. It is extremely rare to see a business that makes millions of dollars in its first year of operation, so do not plan and work towards making that your goal. Steady progress is more attainable, and if your work produces more fruit than expected then that is a bonus. It is always prudent to plan conservatively. Keeping realistic goals and obtainable milestones will keep you motivated as you continue your journey with your business. Franchising strives to create long-term success. It is critical to make sure that your expectations and the typical growth curve of a franchise in the system you are looking at match up.

Preparation = Success

Those that prepare will have much more success than those who wing it. Repetition creates cleaner, more precise ideas. That very fact makes preparation key. Whether it is a presentation that you need to make to an investor or a product that your team is developing, understand the background and the environment you are entering. Analyze the restraints and challenges you will face. Understand the potential good and bad of a situation, and work hard to analyze possible scenarios until you are comfortable moving forward. No one can understand everything, but the more you understand, the more you can anticipate and achieve. Prepare with the help of others too— an extra pair of eyes can be very helpful. Franchise companies understand this, and the repetition of their business model across hundreds of units and many years of experience produces a result that is much more replicable by a new unit in their system.

Preparation and diligence—do your homework and understand all the ins and outs—do not fall in love with the underlying business but understand what makes it successful.

—Lane Fisher Esq., Partner at Fisher Zucker LLC

Leadership Styles

- Is a franchisor supposed to be the leader of its franchisees?
- Are franchisees supposed to govern themselves?
- How does leadership play a role in your business?
- How does an entrepreneur lead?

The successful leadership of an entity requires using the appropriate leadership style for the particular situation at hand. The key leadership styles we will be examining are visionary leadership, coaching leadership, democratic leadership, and authoritative leadership. Each of these styles has their strengths and weaknesses, and finding the right style for a variety of situations will allow you to succeed in almost any venture, franchise or otherwise. Similarly, different franchise systems have different types of leaders. You will want to understand what kind of leader you are and what kind of leadership you are most comfortable working with. Additionally, where the franchise system is in its growth curve is going to play a role in what kind of leader is most appropriate for that particular stage of growth. Many entrepreneurs bring in more seasoned leaders once their company takes off to handle administrative functions that they are not familiar with. Think of the early stage growth of Google when Larry Page and Sergey Brin brought in Eric Schmidt to oversee Google's growth from a start-up company to a more mature endeavor.

Visionary Leaders

Strengths

Visionary leaders focus on coming up with the big picture of a business. They see great value in new, innovative ideas. They want to make their biggest dreams come true, often inspiring their teams to believe in grander visions, and they often want the highest quality work from their team members.

This sort of leadership is the most effective at higher-level positions and during the earliest phases of projects. When involved in start-ups or product development teams, these kinds of leaders can play a key role in boosting the company morale.

Weaknesses

Visionary leaders tend to be scatterbrained. They often feel frustrated when other members of their organizations do not understand their ideas, and they lack details when executing projects.

The Franchisee View

Visionary leaders may create tension in a franchisee-franchisor relationship. Franchisors usually want to keep things the same. Though visionary individuals can create great value when they develop new ideas, it is important to remember that as a franchisee, you are looking to execute a proven business model. There can be some creativity, depending on whom you franchise with, but completely changing a business model is not the purpose of franchising. This sort of leadership style is effective in a franchise model during a crisis or major issues within your franchise unit. Visionary change should be desired and used when the time is right.

Imagine your business is going under water, and you are losing a ton of sales to a new competitor that has come into the fold. It would make sense for you to work with your franchisor to perhaps come up with alternative pricing strategies and creative giveaways to regain market share. However, you do not want to purchase a franchise only to have the model changed to the "idea of the month" at the franchisors whim. That is a dangerous proposition. You are gambling your business to be a test subject.

Coaching Leadership

Strengths

Coaching leaders are all about mentoring employees. They work hard to develop relationships that not only increase value for the company, but for the individuals themselves. They buy into the idea that the "boots on the ground" make a company, rather than just the customers.

These leaders are most effective at handling employee and customer relations. They know when to forgive and what skills their teams lack. They also know where to place individuals to maximize satisfaction and output.

Weaknesses

These kinds of leaders occasionally forget to look at the task at hand. They get so caught up in coaching and nurturing their people that deadlines and goals that aren't hit are viewed as a coaching opportunity. Realizing when their focus needs to change from team building to something else is a trait these leaders may lack.

The Franchisee View

Almost all franchises can excel with this kind of leadership. A decent chunk of the business details are already worked out by the franchisor. Those that can assemble a team and teach other to execute their duties within the franchise unit are of high value. This kind of leadership is most effective outside of crisis situations. Imagine bringing up a cashier to understand the ins and outs of the business, seeing him graduate high school, and becoming a manager at your franchise. As his experiences grows, his loyalty to you grows—you taught him everything he knows!

Democratic Leadership

Strengths

These kinds of leaders thrive off of group support. They are consistently polling to determine what employees think is the best way to handle a situation, and almost everyone within an entity enjoys being around this kind of leader since the employees' opinions are heard and respected.

They are the most effective when the task at hand requires vast amount of buy-in and a multitude of crucial working parts. Sophisticated businesses that have many working parts that produce high value need democratic leaders who can find solutions and run the business in a fashion that keeps key team members positive and engaged.

Weaknesses

This leadership style will never work if employees are stubborn or troublesome. When issues strike, this kind of leader will be looking for a solution that many can agree upon, but often this kind of solution is not at hand. These kinds of leaders occasionally feel unable to fire individuals if they are being unproductive. They view all opinions as valuable, and this may lead to long drawn-out processes to find solutions. Management by committee can bog a process down if the leader is not effective at building consensus and managing the process of decision making.

Franchisee View

A franchise can run off of a democratic model, as long as the franchisee has a multitude of key players that interact to achieve business success. Each business has a different set of priorities and a different strategy to reach the market and obtain customers. Knowing this, it is crucial to understand your business and know when to take opinions, and when not to. Sometimes, you just have to make the tough decisions yourself; you do not have the time or need for a consensus.

This approach is ideal in sophisticated franchises and when big decisions are being made. Having buy-in from all levels of your value chain, especially your franchisor, is crucial. It is important to know when your decisions affect your partners and customers.

Imagine you are deciding to introduce a new product that requires all members of the team to change how they work day in and day out, even just a little bit. If everyone is not on board and excited to make this new product, and some part of the value chain slacks on quality, a customer may get a defective order and end up extremely upset. Having everyone on board is a safety net that increases your quality.

Authoritative Leadership

Strengths

Authoritative leaders set clear goals and expectations, and they create a battle plan to achieve these set expectations. They create lists and objectives that must be met week after week, and though their visions are limited, they tend be very specific. There is usually very little room for mistakes, and tasks get done quickly. There is not much bickering or drawn-out processes. They are also effective at getting buy-in from their team members.

These leaders are the most effective when there are set projects to be completed. They work hard to execute a plan. They are great as managers in the middle to lower levels of an enterprise.

Weaknesses

Sometimes these leaders get so caught up in their duties that they miss bigger opportunities and chances. They almost ignore alternative solutions to problems and work hard to achieve what is at the forefront of their minds. Occasionally, these kinds of leaders burn out, as they tend to overwork themselves to ensure all facets of their plans are executed, even if it means they have to do a lot of the execution.

Franchisee View

These leaders are extremely effective at running franchises because the business model and research is already done by the franchisor. As a franchisee, these leaders take a group of people through the execution of the business model. Whether one is in crisis-management or prosperous times, authoritative leaders can be effective at owning franchises.

Franchise Overview

It is vital to remember that all franchises are different and all people are different. Some franchises may require vastly different kinds of leaders at vastly different times. It is up to you to figure out and decide which leadership style works in your franchise situation. There will be a trial-and-error period with mistakes—no matter how much preparation the franchisor gives you, there is no such thing as perfect advice.

Summary

While there is not a magic formula to being an entrepreneur, there are ten traits that successful leaders share to various degrees.

1. Patience
2. Satisfaction
3. Organization
4. Discipline
5. A Reflective-Nature
6. Creativity
7. Curiosity
8. Risk Calculation
9. Goal Orientation
10. Ability to Adjust One's Leadership Styles

The inability to perfectly define leadership is the beauty of a business enterprise—entrepreneurs get a chance to truly discover who they are, where their weaknesses lie, and lead a business to prosperity. Each struggle is a lesson that empowers us to understand what new leadership styles we need to develop to succeed in our chosen fields. These ideas we learn today are mere starting points for the grander journey to our success.

I view joy as the content of success. If I am satisfied with what I have done with my day, I am successful. There is not a goal that needs to be reached to define my worth. The ability to innovate, and make others succeed is success enough. At the end of the day, I share my success, I rejoice in the success of others, I enjoy my family and friends, and I have little to worry over.

—Art Husami, E.A., C.F.P., C.I.M.A.

CEO, Husami & Associates

CHAPTER 4 - WEALTH IN AMERICA

That night, when Mark went home and talked about this new opportunity, his wife gave him a small smile. He had missed that smile for the longest time, and he felt it would be appropriate to at least consider talking to this company.

He sent Marina's CEO, Dr. Garret, an email requesting to hear more about the company and opportunities to work with it. Within hours, Dr. Garret sent him an eloquent response, and requested an interview the next day in the afternoon. Mark eagerly agreed.

The next day promised to be a fantastic start to his new life. He had time to spend eating breakfast with his wife, and he drove his daughter to fifth grade. The moments he relished with them seemed so much more powerful.

As the afternoon unfolded, he drove carefully to Green Lake Park. It was a light industrial park with small businesses of all kinds as tenants. He pulled up to the location and the words "Marina Technology" in vinyl lettering on the door heralded the start of a new venture. He took a deep breath. He had worked for a Fortune 500 company with locations around the world. He remembered the sense of pride when he saw his company's products on store shelves and on TV. It seemed like he had come a long way from his dreams of being a global executive to walking through the door of "Marina

Technology."

When he entered the room, he noticed the whole place felt like it was furnished from a second- hand store. His gut made him feel a bit uncomfortable, but he trudged forward and sat near the front desk. Within moments he saw a taller, robust figure enter the room. The figure's eyes focused on Mark.

"You are Mark. Am I correct in this assumption?" the figure asked.

"Yes. Are you Dr. Garret?" Mark replied

"Of course I am. Let's head over to my office."

Mark followed Dr. Garret to a cramped office space with little legroom. Inside it was a small refrigerator that radiated a white glow, while the rest of the room had darker features that overpowered any upbeat presence.

"So Mark, I understand you have many abilities in the IT sector. I have seen your resume online, and your LinkedIn profile provides a lot of strong recommendations. I've developed a Marina management system for aquariums and lake-and water-based zoos. I need someone to handle the technology and meet with clients and explain it to them." After a round of perfunctory interview questions, it was clear that he was overqualified, but he was offered the job. Since it was a start-up, he could always make it sound bigger than it was on his resume and say that he was a consultant. Hopefully, it wouldn't hurt his chances at another job if something better came along.

Mark was surprised with how quick Dr. Garret offered him a job. Nervous, but determined not to let down his wife, Mark said, "I can start tomorrow."

"Great. You'll be paid a $45,000 salary. I know it's less than what you were making, but as we grow, you'll have the ability to grow as well. Your office is across the hall."

"Thanks, Dr. Garret. I'll see you tomorrow."

Mark went home to share the good news. His wife responded with the most incredible demeanor, and even his daughter noticed the positive vibe in the room. Even though he was making the kind of money he made in his twenties, he had something to do. He felt productive. Something better would come along and, who knows, maybe Marina Technology would hit the big time.

What is wealth in America? Who are the wealthy? How do you become wealthy? Here is a very simple piece of advice that will help you on your road to wealth: create a surplus. Keep more than you spend and make it grow faster over time than the rise in the cost of things you can buy with it.

There is no subtler, no surer means of overturning the existing basis of society than to debauch the currency. The process engages all the hidden forces of economic law on the side of destruction, and does it in a manner which not one man in a million is able to diagnose.

—John Maynard Keynes, father of macroeconomics

Consumer Price Index

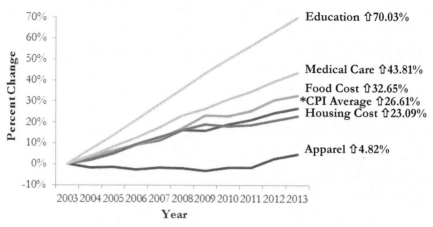

Education ⇑70.03%

Medical Care ⇑43.81%

Food Cost ⇑32.65%
*CPI Average ⇑26.61%
Housing Cost ⇑23.09%

Apparel ⇑4.82%

*CPI Average includes all categories, some not shown

Source: US Bureau of Labor Statistics January 2003=Base Year

The above chart shows the rise in costs for certain goods in the U.S. Think back to your own past. How much did a year of college cost? What was the percentage of a year's tuition to the average income when you were attending your undergraduate institution? What is it now? How much did a first-class stamp cost? How about a gallon of gas? When you got your first car, how much did a gallon of gas cost? In 1975, the average cost of a new car was $4,250. Median income in 1975 was $33,148. A new car cost about 13% of one's yearly income. In 2011, the average car cost about $30,000 and the median income for that year was about $50,502. A new car cost about 59% of one's yearly income. To put that into perspective, you needed to work from January 1st until February 17th in 1975 to buy a car. In 2011, to purchase the same car, you would have worked from January 1st to August 3rd. That is the reality of inflation. For the vast majority of the population, the income generated by working as an employee does not keep pace with cost increases. The standard of living has dropped.

The past several years in the United States have seen the federal government responding to the downturn in the economy through quantitative easing. Cheap money has been made available, and cheap money inevitably leads to inflation. As prices increase and purchasing power decreases, the hardest hit are those who have no ability to adjust. If you are living on fixed income or have a job in which your wage increases do not at least keep up with inflation, you are not able to purchase as much each year. In effect, you are getting poorer. Governments have done this many times over history in order to attain financial gain at the expense of their citizens. By reducing the value of the currency, a government can create inflation, allowing the government to pay off their debt. However, the purchasing power of the citizens is reduced. This is a direct and forced transfer of wealth from those who have accumulated assets by a government intent on changing the status quo.

One of the key advantages of owning a business is that you are able to pass along price increases to your consumers, as well as keep ahead of the inflation curve. If you are collecting a paycheck, you are relying upon the benevolence of your employer to keep you and your family ahead of the inflation curve. Is your employer benevolent?

Quantitative easing is not a new phenomenon. When currency was gold or silver, the value of the coins would be debased, or decreased, to achieve this aim. In Roman times, the value of Denarius gradually decreased as the government decreased the size and silver content of the coin. Originally, the coin was almost pure silver. Over time, the coin became 2 percent silver and the rest base metal. Take a look at a U.S. Quarter; the edges are ridged or "reeded." When coins were solid precious metal, these ridges prevented people from filing down or "clipping" the coins to keep an amount of the precious metal and pass off the coin at its full value. Originally, a U.S. Quarter was solid silver; today, the U.S. Quarter is 75 percent copper and 25 percent nickel and costs about 7.5 cents to manufacture. Even though the metal has been completely debased, the ridges still remain for aesthetic purposes. The currency has been debased legally. What the government does not want its citizens to do, it can do by law. The citizenry just can't see what they have done because the coins look the same.

With the advent of paper currency, the way to debase it is to simply crank up the presses and print more. This has effects that are just as disastrous. After World War I, Germany was obliged to pay reparations to the victors. This crippled its economy and lead to quantitative easing through the printing of more money. Inflation got so out of hand that eventually it took a wheelbarrow full of money to buy a loaf of bread. "My father was a lawyer," says Walter Levy, an internationally known German-born oil consultant in New York, "and he had taken out an insurance policy in 1903, and every month he had made the payments faithfully. It was a twenty-year policy, and when it came due, he cashed it in and bought a single loaf of bread."

Owning a business is a hedge against inflation and a hedge against your economic independence being taken away from you. If you own a business, and inflation is 4 percent a year, you can increase your prices by 5 percent and have a 1 percent increase in your real earnings. You control this. It is very difficult to ask your boss for a 5 percent increase just because inflation is occurring.

Think of the companies that can pass along price increases and customers continue to buy their products, whether they like the price or not. This is pricing power. Companies like Disney and Coca-Cola can pass along cost increases. Can the franchise you are looking at do the same?

Just as you purchase insurance to protect against unforeseen calamities, purchasing a business is a way to protect against future pricing that you currently have no control over.

Serve the masses, eat with the classes. Serve the classes, eat with the masses.

—Anonymous

I will never forget the lady who told me this. I was in my early twenties, running a jewelry business on the island of Santorini, Greece. I met very interesting people, and I loved learning about their backgrounds and their stories. I still do! One of my favorite questions to ask them was "How did you become successful?" The answers tended to fall into certain categories, and the people often had similar outlooks on life. It was a high-end jewelry business, and the clientele who could afford to purchase our baubles were well-off. They tended to be older, and I learned some very fascinating life lessons from these folks. Most had made their money themselves. They were not born into wealth. Most were not jet-setters. There were two categories that everyone seemed to fall into: those who were content with their life decisions and those who seemed to have regrets. Many of those with regrets were the ones who were amazed that I was in my twenties, living on a Greek island, running a business, and having a great time. They would usually say, "I wish I had done something like this when I was younger." People in the group without regrets would usually ask me questions about who I was and then share what they did when they were younger. Sometimes I found myself thinking, "Wow, I want to do that!"

How does this correlate to wealth? Wealth is not simply a pile of cash—it is the life experiences that freedom and independence bring. A big factor in achieving independence is being able to control your time. Think of the things you have stressed out about in the past. In hindsight, they probably seem relatively small. At the very end, most of the regrets that people have tend to be around areas that they could have controlled. Here are a few culprits that I have heard countless people talk about over the years that motivated their decision to buy a business:

1. I spend too much time at work

    Think about the number of hours you have spent at work. Over half of U.S. knowledge workers check their work e-mail in bed. Do you? More than half check their work e-mail on vacation. Over a third checks their work e-mail at the family dinner. More than two-thirds of these workers cannot go to sleep without checking their e-mail one last time. The workers that check their e-mail on vacation often make work calls while on vacation. The top reasons for staying "plugged in" and "connected" is "I was worried my boss would get angry and this would impact my future with the company" or "I was worried I would fall behind" or "my team needed me". This is living in fear and with an inflated ego.

Would these sophisticated i-Phone and Blackberry toting employees look askance at the Amazonian tribesman who looks into the sky every night and makes ritualistic hand gestures to ward off fiery rocks that shoot down from the heavens and destroy the earth? Of course they would. How silly of these tribes-people. You can't control a meteor apocalypse through hand gestures. Those tribes-people would look same way at us diligently hunched over our phones while our kids play in the surf. Can you really ward off losing your job or falling behind by taking time out of your vacation to work? Just ask anyone from Enron, Lehman Brothers or Bear Stearns. The majority of them were hard working, honest employees who fall victim to the actions of their leaders.

Does your "team" really need you that badly that email guidance from you saves the day? Probably not. Americans work longer hours, take less vacation, and retire later than many people around the world. Would you rather spend time with your family but feel that if you are not the model employee, you might get fired? Is your "work family" more important than your real family? When you are on your deathbed, will that e-mail really be something you will reflect back upon with satisfaction?

2. I am worried about the risk

No one likes to fail. But you will never win if you do not put yourself in a place of risk. We are all going to die eventually. Take a risk. Who knows, you might win. If you control your actions and activities you will most certainly influence the outcome of your behaviors. The first step to winning is engaging in the right activities. If you control the activities, you control the outcome. Are you waiting for the right moment to open a business? Is there such a thing as the right moment?

3. I do not love my job, but they pay me well

How many people do you know who love their jobs? I do not mean the sycophants who pretend to love their work in front of the bosses—I mean really love their job. Not many. And most do not do anything about it. If you love your job, you will probably love your life.

How do you measure wealth? What is a good benchmark? How much should you be worth right now? In *The Millionaire Next Door*, authors Thomas J. Stanley and William D. Danko have a good rule of thumb that is remarkably accurate at analyzing net worth in relation to one's age and income level:

"Multiply your age times your realized pre-tax annual household income from all sources except inheritances. Divide by ten. This, less any inherited wealth is what your net worth should be."

For example, Bob is forty-seven years old, makes $125,000 a year, and has investments that generate another $10,000 for a total income of $135,000. To figure out his net worth, he would multiply $135,000 by 47 to get $6,345,000. Dividing by ten shows his net worth should be $634,500. If his wife works, perform the same calculations with her information and add it to Bob's amount. This calculation is for average individuals in this demographic. If Bob had a net worth of $1,200,000, he would be an above-average accumulator of wealth. If he had a $300,000 net worth, he would be a below-average accumulator. Remember, he is making $125,000 a year.

Where is his money going?

Making a large amount of income is not the key—saving it is. Seventy-eight percent of NFL players are bankrupt or in severe financial distress within two years of leaving their profession. Why? They make a lot of money, but it comes fast and at an early age. Most have no experience in financial budgeting. The majority of the wealthy in this country become wealthy by budgeting and controlling their expenses. Does your household operate on an annual budget?

1. Do you know how much your family spends each year for food, clothing, and shelter?
2. Do you have a clearly defined set of financial goals, including daily, weekly, monthly, annual, and lifetime?
3. Do you spend a lot of time planning your financial future?

Does this sound like a business? It should. It is the economics of your personal family wealth. Economics is a Greek word derived from 'oikos' or house (οικοσ) while 'nomos' (νομοσ) is the study of law, statutes or ordinances. Economics (οικονομια) is the branch of knowledge concerned with the production, consumption, and transfer of wealth but the original meaning is really the "law of the house". In fact, the Greek word for family is 'oikogenia' (οικογενεια) or a "home across the generations". I take the meaning of these words to signify the proper allocation and planning of household wealth for the long-term security and benefit of the family.

If you did not grow up this way or have not developed these habits as fully as you would like, a franchise is a good way to inject discipline into your financial life. Any quality franchise is going to have a training program and a business development program where you are going to create a budget. The franchisor will help you track your actual expenses versus budgeted expenses on a regular basis in order to help your business grow. The more you grow, the more you and the franchisor make, since the franchisor's income is mostly dependent upon the royalty that you pay them. Most franchisors will assign a corporate individual to your business whose job is to get to know your business and be your coach. Very often, the habits you create by learning to operate within the franchise business will spill over to your personal life. This can be a great asset to your life.

Taxes and Time

Most people want to be comfortably wealthy and enjoy independence. In fact, most of the people I have spoken with over the years have similar goals around wealth accumulation and independence even if the absolute amounts are not the same. Many people do not have written goals. There is indisputable evidence that the positive effect of written goals is profound. Those who write down their goals accomplish significantly more than those who do not.

Ask just about anybody if they want to be wealthy. Most people will say yes. However, most people do not want to spend the time, energy, and resources to enhance their opportunity to achieve this goal. Be introspective for a minute. What kind of employee are you? What kind of person are you? When confronted with an obstacle, do you give up readily, or do you find a way to go around it, through it, under it, or over it?

Owning a business is really about being in the business of you. By that I mean you looking out for you and your best interests. Nobody is going to care about your money and time as much as you are. Think about how much time you spend at work, how much brain share work consumes. If you own your business, every activity that you undertake is benefiting you. Every additional hour you spend working is benefiting you. Every customer you go to see is benefiting you. Many business owners say they work harder than they ever had when starting their businesses, but it does not feel like work because everything they do is for a purpose that they can connect with— making their future a better place. Do you have that kind of passion at your current job? When you work hard, do you feel resentful? Have you felt that you have created a lot of wealth and equity for your company, but nothing is coming back to you?

If you have a discipline around investing and planning your

financial future, you are more likely to achieve wealth. People who treat their wealth as a business tend to spend time on it. People who do not treat it as such tend to spend their time on other activities and achieve less. Work is an important factor here. There is a correlation between being self-employed and time spent planning investment strategies, as opposed to the time spent on investments by employees. The self-employed, even those with middle incomes, typically integrate investment planning into their work lives. Most employees have a set of job- related tasks that are independent of planning their investment strategies. If you are an employee, do you spend time analyzing your portfolio at work? Would your boss be supportive of that activity?

There is a different mindset between the employed and the self-employed. Employees tend to view self-employment as risky. Why? What is causing the risk? Typical answers are "the economy is not good right now" or "my kids are going to be going to college" or "my friend said that owning a business is tough." There are a million answers. All of them tend to stem from fear.

Business owners tend to view being employed by someone else as risky. Why? There tends to be one answer. "I am dependent upon the decisions of someone else." There were a lot of smart, hardworking employees at Enron, MCI, Bear Stearns, Lehman Brothers, and countless other "safe," "solid" companies. They lost their jobs due to circumstances out of their control. Perhaps you have lost your job to circumstances out of your control. As an employee, your income is coming from one source. As a business owner, you have hundreds of sources of income—your clients. If one client does not work out, you can always go and find others to replace that client.

Being self-employed is hard work. So is being an employee. How many hours do you work a week? If you are like most of the employee readers of this book, you have probably worked fifty to seventy hours a week and travelled significantly. You work every bit as hard as a business owner. Most employees who are making upper-five- or lower-six-digit salaries usually spend most of their time and energy on their jobs. How many times have you dragged yourself home after a week on the road? How often did your exertions that week move your family's financial needle forward? Did you get to determine where your time would be spent, or did you perform a task because the boss told you to go and do something? You did not write your job description. You probably have some kind of yearly goals that were "agreed upon" by you and your manager, and then you review them at the end of the year when you discuss your "performance."

The self-employed, by contrast, do write their own job descriptions, and they tend to have very significant occupation goals; one of them is to become financially independent. They are independent in their actions, and their work is not graded by a supervisor. It is graded by the market. If they do well, their bank account grows. It follows that the self-employed actively seek out and spend time on activities that further their independence. If you are an employee, you are dependent upon someone else. Do not kid yourself. If you are dependent on someone else, it is likely that you have slowly, over time, become less self-reliant in planning your investments. Think about how much control you have over your 401k investments. You can choose from a menu of predetermined options. As an employee, you have the illusion of choice in many aspects of your working life. As Thomas Ward wrote, "Where to elect there is but one, / 'Tis Hobson's choice—take that, or none."

People with significant wealth tend to hold more of their wealth in assets that appreciate over time, such as businesses and real estate. This requires planning and foresight. These types of assets tend to be the building blocks of significant wealth. People with lower amounts of wealth tend to hold their wealth in cash or near-cash assets that can be liquidated quickly in case of "an emergency." These people tend to also hold a greater percentage of their wealth in automobiles and items that depreciate. Which type of person are you? Which would you like to be? When Ray Kroc started franchising McDonald's, he learned that the owner-operator must be an entrepreneur who is willing to stake everything he owns for a chance to operate the business. To this day, the franchisee is required to work full time in the management of the restaurant. Ray Kroc knew that holding ones' wealth in assets that require planning and hard work encourages behaviors that lead to success.

Either way, as an employee or as a business owner, you will work hard and have risk. Risk that you can control and act independently to reduce is calculated risk. Rolling up your sleeves and making it happen is the American way. As Yoda said, "Try not. Do! Or do not. There is no try."

Who are the affluent? Who are the wealthy in this country?

The average American household has a net worth of about $100,000. However, two-thirds of that amount is contained in home equity. The average household income in the U.S. in 2011 was $50,502. The top 10 percent had incomes exceeding $100,000. The top 5 percent of households had incomes exceeding $166,200 and the top 1.5 percent had incomes exceeding $250,000. The top 1 percent of the country controlled 42 percent of all financial wealth.

Household Income Distribution

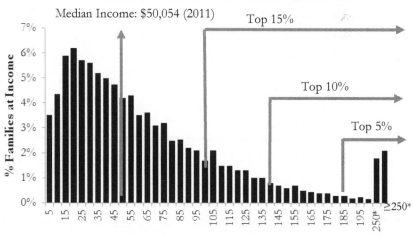

Household Income ($5,000 Categories)

*Ten Income Brackets Wide
** All Incomes ≥250

Twenty percent of the affluent are retirees. Of the remaining eighty percent, more than two-thirds are self-employed owners of businesses. Simply put, most of the affluent in America are business owners, including self-employed professionals. To put this into perspective, in America, fewer than one in five households is headed by a self-employed business owner, but these self-employed people are four times more likely to be millionaires than those who work for others.

What is the true measure of wealth? Is it success and independence? Wealth can only be measured in personal terms, but there are elements common to all of us. I propose that success is enjoying what you do to such a degree that you cannot wait to get out of bed in the morning and go do it. You provide value and good to your community and are recognized and rewarded for it. The fear of not being in control of your economic destiny subsides as you create a surplus that will outlast your needs. The material rewards are there, but over time, they become less important, and you focus on being able to spend time on the pursuits that are most important to you, whether that is family, philanthropy or other matters. Over time, your personal and business life blends to such a degree that you do the things you love and love the things you do. I believe this is the key to wealth, and that is why business owners are so abundant in the ranks of the wealthy in this country.

CHAPTER 5- OWNING A BUSINESS

Going to work the next morning was a great change of pace for Mark. He noticed his spirit was uplifted, and he had an opportunity to make a great first impression. As he entered his office, he noticed how much smaller it was than he expected. There was a small note on his desk.

The note read, "Mark. Dr. Garret here. Just wanted to let you know that I have sent a task list to your work e-mail. Your work e-mail should automatically load when you log on to the desktop."

Mark started his computer and opened his e-mail. What he saw shocked him—the task list was a mere list of scripts he had to code. It made no sense—wasn't he a VP in the company? Why wasn't he meeting with clients, or helping employees achieve success? Where was the team of people he could lead?

Frustrated, Mark walked to Dr. Garret's office.

Mark complained, "Dr. Garrett—I was wondering why my task list, as you called it, has a bunch of coding that I need to do. Don't you have someone doing this for you?"

"Mark, my man—understand one thing. You are the manager, and the worker. We all have to pitch in here with whatever is needed, coding what clients want during the day, and meeting the clients at night. I've already met with a marina that needs some software for

HR management. They need very specific features. You have two work days to get that done—then we need to meet him again tomorrow night."

Mark stood puzzled at his ridiculous demands. Agitated, he made his way back to his desk. Hour after hour, he coded line by line for the software package he needed to make. Assembling the code went well into the night, and he went home exhausted.

His wife noticed how unhappy he looked but just ignored it. The next day at work, Mark spent a good eleven hours coding software. He heard a hard knock at his door.

"Mark, what are you doing? Get out here right now! The client is waiting for us in the lobby— bring your software on a flash drive."

Mark obeyed his orders and got himself ready. Slowly he walked to the lobby. A pale, staunch character paced back and forth.

"Hi, I'm Roger, the owner of the Seattle Marina. I hope the software package I requested is ready as to my specifications."

Mark nodded, and handed him the flash drive. "Take a look for yourself." Within moments, Roger had the package loaded up onto his computer. Roger looked through it and frowned.

Roger calmly stated, "It's ok. It just doesn't have any of the colors I want. And the e-mail I sent you one hour ago with extra changes—none of those have been implemented yet. I don't think I want this…"

Mark was about to explode—he hadn't checked his e-mail in a while, but regardless of what the demands were, it would have been impossible to script so much code in such a short manner of time. This whole job, and working this way, was getting ridiculous.

Dr. Garrett was getting impatient with what he was hearing from Sam and practically screamed, "Mark! I can't believe you didn't check your e-mail and get this done. I truly apologize, Roger, for the lack of quality. I'll make sure it is fixed before Mark heads home for the day."

Mark couldn't stand it from then on. Calmly, but sternly, he stated, "I'm done, Dr. Garrett. Not only is this not what I signed up for, but I wasn't expecting to be coding for twenty-four hours in a span of two days. You can write your own code!"

Mark stormed out of the office and headed home. As he headed to his car, a wrapped van pulled into the space next to him. The wrap made the van look like a giant, moving billboard, and Mark had heard of the company before. He thought it was a franchise. The van door opened, and a man about Mark's age got out. He was wearing an oxford shirt and carried a clipboard. Mark looked at him, said good morning, and then did a double take. It was his friend Sam. Sam used to be the controller for one of the divisions and was laid off during the first round of layoffs a few years ago.

"Sam! What are you doing? Is this your business?" It was. Sam had purchased a franchise that provided services to small businesses. Sam looked great—full of life and vigor. He told Mark that it had not been easy getting started, but now he had clients and he enjoyed what he was doing. He gave Mark his card and said, "Call me, we can talk more about it. I have a client I need to see. Can't be late!"

Mark had always wanted to start a business from a young age and thought, if Sam could do it, why couldn't he? A franchise. What an interesting concept. He had never thought of that.

When Mark went home, he spilled the news to his wife.

"I quit my job."

Mark's wife just stared blankly at him and walked upstairs to bed. She didn't say a word. Mark knew he had to do something, and he just kept thinking of his experience at Marina Technology. Maybe it was time to consider calling Sam and asking him how he did it and to get some advice. He would need some input. Was working for yourself even a worthwhile proposition? Was it worth the risk? An awkward mixture of fear and motivation overcame him.

Owning your own business is owning your destiny; you are not going to be a millionaire if you are not going to work hard. You have to look at yourself and know you have to dedicate the time to it. Make it part of your life.

—John Georgedakis
Owner of All My Sons Moving and Storage of Raleigh, NC

When you were a kid, perhaps you dreamed of being a firefighter, astronaut, president, or superhero. Kids want to be something that correlates to the specific activities that they are constantly exposed to. If you ask kids what they want to be, you will seldom hear that they want to be entrepreneurs or a middle managers in a Fortune 1000 company. When we look at statistics, there are approximately 7,396,628 non-farm businesses in the United States. Therefore, one in every 42 Americans owns his or her own business. About 2.3% of the population can call themselves a true business owner. The vast majority of Americans are employees; this is what is comfortable to the masses. But after you have worked for a firm for ten or twenty years, what is your identity? Does this answer change once you are retired or unemployed? After all the years of belonging to a group of people who get up in the morning, go to the same building, and do similar tasks, you have been given an identity: name, age, title, and company. You go from John, eighteen, student at a university, to John, twenty-five, full-time mechanical engineer. We go from entity to entity depending on where we are exerting our energy at the moment. There is a key difference to recognize—we go from paying schools for their time to asking companies to rent our time. That is a job at its core—you renting out your time. This section will give you more tools and knowledge to help you decide whether business ownership or employment is right for you.

One of the biggest mistakes we hear is not necessarily about getting into the wrong franchise—it's about the fact that going into business at all was just not for them.

—Jania Bailey, President and COO of FranNet

We have examined the implications of business ownership in reference to wealth. This chapter examines the effects of business ownership on personal finances in comparison to employment.

Tax Breaks

As a business owner, you are offered additional opportunities to reduce your tax burden. Business expenses such as advertising, utilities, and supplies can be deducted as current business expenses. These expenses often will overlap with your personal life. If your business expenses are based on something you would do anyway, you may be able to deduct purchases you would make whether or not you run a business. It is important to make sure that the expense is actually necessary to the success of your business. It is important to keep records of these expenses in the event of an IRS audit.
Examples:

- If you pick up the tab from entertaining a current or prospective client, you may deduct 50 percent of the cost if it related to the business and business is discussed or if it is associated with the business (immediately before or after a meeting).

- If you use your car for business or your business owns vehicles, you may receive deductions for some of the costs for keeping these vehicles on the road. If your car is used for both professional and personal life, then only the business use is tax deductible.

- Professional fees that you pay to accountants, lawyers, or consultants can be deducted in the year.

When you work for a company, you receive your income after taxes have already been subtracted. Your income is then taxed again when you spend it on your personal expenses. Owning your own company allows you to deduct the business portion of your expenses from your taxes so that your income from your business is not taxed twice. More information on corporate structures and their tax advantages is provided in chapter 17.

Who makes more money—Entrepreneur or Employee?

We can evaluate this in the case of the employee. This employee, a mechanical engineer, has no risk, no debt, and invests very little if he chooses to work for a firm. Say he makes $150,000 dollars his first year. From a short-term standpoint, it is clearly in the employees' favor to stick with his job versus an entrepreneur starting out with a business that generates $30,000 for the entrepreneur. The opportunity of making $30,000 in owner benefit is outweighed by the employee's $150,000 salary. There are higher expenses in the first year of ownership for the entrepreneur. Still, there are the tax benefits to consider. A business owner can purchase his vehicle directly through the business, while the employee has to pay for it from his taxed income. For year two, the benefits still favor the employee; however, they begin to even out. The business owner has done better in raising his gross revenue and is continuing to build his equity. He has more than doubled his owner benefit, while the employee is still making a six-figure salary.

Here is a table to show the differences between being a business owner and an employee:

	Entrepreneur	Business Equity	Employee	Business Equity
Startup Investment	$225,000	$225,000	$0	$0
Year 1	$30,000 Owner Benefit (10% Net)	$300,000	$150,000 Salary	$0
Year 2	$78,750 Owner Benefit (15% Net)	$525,000	$157,500 Salary	$0
Year 3	$135,000 Owner Benefit (20% Net)	$675,000	$162,000 Salary	$0

At the end of these three years what do the entrepreneur and employee have to show for their work?

The mechanical engineering position has an asset value of zero at the end of three years. He does not own the office, the computer, or the job. The entrepreneur, on the other hand, has built a business that is worth more than his investment of $225,000. His business is worth almost $675,000. While owners take on more risk to create a business, they are able to generate assets and create equity for themselves.

The owner gets the benefits of cash flow, tax benefits, and asset creation.

ROCK 2 – UNDERSTANDING THE FRANCHISOR

Mark called up his friend Sam. After catching up for a little bit, Mark got into the meat of his problems.

"Sam, I'll be honest with you. I'm a bit lost at the moment. I got fired and spent months trying to find a job. When you saw me the other day, I had just quit the crappy job I did find. After seeing you the other day, I am thinking of starting a new business. Can you help me? How did you do it?" Mark asked.

"Well, I had the same challenges that you did. I couldn't find anything good, and what I did find was paying a pittance. I knew I wanted to do something but didn't want to reinvent the wheel. I looked at a bunch of different franchise companies and found the one that made the most sense. It's not easy, but it sure is better than going around begging for a job. Maybe you should consider buying a franchise," Sam replied.

CHAPTER 6 - DESCRIBING THE FRANCHISOR SYSTEM

The idea of selling a business model has been around for hundreds of years. During the Middle Ages, local leaders would designate and teach certain duties to specific people in their locale. This could mean that only one individual would run a fair or operate a windmill. Kings at the time caught on to this idea of providing a business model to certain segments of the population. They then "franchised" functions of the kingdom to certain districts under their domain, and some nobles even allowed individuals to apply to serve certain functions.

In the 1840s, German breweries gave taverns exclusive rights to sell their beers. This relationship is the first time the world caught a glimpse of modern franchising. In America, Albert Singer is considered the father of the franchise model. In 1851, he took his Singer Sewing Machine Industry and brought it to the United States, setting up satellite companies to sell his sewing machines. He was one of the first individuals to actually create written contracts for franchising, and his legal documentation became the foundation for many of the legal documents that are used today.

As franchising has grown to encompass over thousands of concepts across multiple industry segments, the International Franchising Association (IFA) has grown to be the leading association of franchisors and the governing body of franchising in the world. This influential organization is located in Washington, D.C. and works tirelessly to promote franchising throughout the world. Stephen Caldeira, 2012 President of the IFA, describes the mission of the IFA as "protecting, enhancing and promoting franchising. It is all about government relations and public policy, media and public relations, and professional development and education." Every franchisor of note is a member of the IFA. It is an organization that you should make sure any franchise that you are working with belongs to.

How has franchising progressed?

Franchising has progressed to become a key tool used in various sectors of the economy, from the government to private enterprises. The use of a franchise model ensures replicability, compliance, stability, and efficiency.

The private sector champions franchises as an effective way to expand a product's reach. Franchising is now available in almost any industry you can think of.

Understanding what you are buying

Buying a franchise is an asset acquisition along with a partnership. While many businesses are out there to sell you tangible goods or a service, a franchise is selling you an idea. Many universities have studied this approach to business, and the M.I.T. Sloan School of Management study entitled "Do Some Business Models Perform Better than Others? A Study of the 1000 Largest US Firms" by Weill, Malone and D'Urso, classified businesses through two dimensions. The first dimension classifies what is being sold by the enterprise, leading to four basic business models: Creator, Distributor, Landlord, and Broker. The second dimension determines what types of assets are being sold and distinguishes among four important asset types: physical, financial, intangible, and human. A franchisor is the creator and provider of an intangible asset. The parent company in this case is the entrepreneur, as the parent company has created the business plan and knows how to run the business. Those running the parent company have the experience they are willing to share, and in return for some equity and/or cash, they are providing you the intellectual property, connections, and support network to potentially make the enterprise a success.

Why Do Companies Franchise?

1. To Reduce Market Risk

   The risk of expanding a business is usually very high. Entering unfamiliar markets will certainly result in some learning curve, failure, and struggles. By having other individuals start businesses under your domain, a franchise effectively reduces its risk of failure in an enterprise while continuing to grow.

2. To Increase Capital Reserves and Working Capital

   All franchise deals will have some sort of up-front payment to the franchisor and a continuing payment known as a royalty. Most franchisors will charge a royalty on revenues generated by the operation of the business either the gross revenues or some other formula that is spelled out in the agreement.

3. To Attract High-Net-Worth Investors and High Potential Partners to the Company

   People are the backbone of any enterprise. Jim Collins, the author of *Good to Great*, could not have said it better when he stated, "A company should limit its growth based on its ability to attract enough of the right people." By providing a franchise option, intelligent, high-net-worth individuals have the opportunity not only to run a business and experience profits, but at the same time to contribute to the positive image of the parent company. Quality franchisors are always on the lookout for skilled and capable individuals to own their franchised operations. It is very common to see franchisees go on to hold significant posts within the leadership of a franchise system.

4. To Expand in a Timely Fashion

    Competition is rampant in many of the industries that have franchising wings. The ability not just to grow but grow quickly within an area is key to gaining footholds in markets. A company without large outside investment will find it tough to expand quickly, and the franchise model creates a large funding source through expedient expansion and investment. It allows companies to capitalize on trends and grow in the U.S. economy.

Why Do Companies Choose Not to Franchise?

1. Desire to better protect intellectual property and contacts

    All companies that franchise assume the risk of giving away intellectual property, techniques, and contacts. No matter how much security and how many clauses are stuffed into a contract with a franchisee, unscrupulous individuals will find ways to use techniques and intellectual property in ventures outside of the franchise. There are countless examples of pizza companies that are started by former pizza franchise owners. These companies use tactics and experiences gained from working with a franchise to their advantage. They may also contact the suppliers that they worked with while working as a franchise and use those contacts to supply for their new business. None of this is necessarily illegal if done properly, but it is a real risk for franchisors.

2. Create an overall higher profit per unit potential

    Franchisors only pull in a percentage of revenues or a fee from their franchisees. However, a company that owns all of its franchised entities will pull in 100 percent of the revenues from those auxiliary entities. This does not mean that every auxiliary entity that a company starts and staffs will be profitable in the first place—hence the word potential. There are even examples of companies that buy back their franchises to secure more revenue streams.

3. Do not have high enough margins to attract franchisees

A franchisee requires significant net margins on top of any fees it owes to a franchisor. If the business itself does not produce these kinds of margins, potential franchisees will walk away. Ensuring that expansion can create these kinds of margins, or already having these margins in place, is crucial.

4. Inadequate staffing and reserves to oversee expansions

Any new operation requires new personnel and excess cash. The skill sets needed to run a company are not the same skill sets needed to teach others to run it the same way. Very few individuals have the ability to both teach and execute effectively. This means that a company who does not have the resources, both physical and intellectual, to manage new locations should not franchise. Plus, with any expansion, there is some risk of loss to the core business. If a franchised unit does something ill-advised and hurts the reputation of the core company, there will be losses involved for all locations, including the core entity. This fact makes excess cash necessary before trusting others to run the business.

5. Too Specialized of a Niche

This is a rare occurrence, but sometimes a business is so specialized and specific that there is not enough demand in the world for franchising to make sense.

What Exactly am I Buying?

When you purchase a franchise, you are acquiring two distinct but important items.

1. The Business Plan

    This is the nuts and bolts of the enterprise. Questions regarding how many employees you need to hire, how the store should look, and so on, are answered within the context of the business plan. Some franchises make this plan somewhat flexible, while others are extremely strict. It all depends on the franchisor's orientation, and this will be further discussed in Chapter 15: The Franchise Disclosure Document FDD.

2. The License

    This is the legal right to use the franchisor's logo and products in your new place of business. This documentation will keep your business safe from trademark and licensing suits as long as all other aspects of the franchisor-franchisee agreement are upheld.

Why Do People Buy Franchises?

1. Successful Record

    All effective franchises have already grown and produced wealth for the parent company and other business units. It is generally true that a business model in one area can work in other areas with tweaks to match the local environment.

2. Brand Recognition

    Quick—when you think of a place that sells hamburgers, what do you think of? How about donuts? You probably thought of McDonald's or Burger King and Dunkin' Donuts or Krispy Kreme. When you think of McDonald's, almost everyone will think of a giant yellow "M." If I say the name Ace, referring to the hardware store, many of you will state the phrase "the helpful place." Many of the entities that are franchised have some brand recognition in their locales. This increases customer trust and can result in more sales than starting a business from scratch that has no reputation.

3. Training

Most successful franchises have effective training programs to speed up your own business success. These programs range from weekend retreats to online seminars, and all of them can boost the effectiveness of your franchise.

4. National Marketing

Quality franchise companies either offer tools for marketing or run national marketing campaigns themselves. Getting nationally recognized attention is easier when one central entity is handling most of the promotion. It keeps messages consistent and allows for building a brand. Even franchises that do not have the size or capital to run national marketing campaigns will usually provide you with the tools to market within your own territory. Whether it is assistance in negotiating ads on local television and newspapers or ideas and techniques to make flyers, franchisors may be available to assist in building your franchise's image to the customer base you serve.

5. Operational Support

All franchises have some rules and regulations on how your company must operate. Franchise companies evaluate and improve these methods, and full-time employees of the franchise companies provide support to all franchisees to keep their businesses running at peak performance. If you are willing to maintain operations using the techniques outlined by the franchisee, you can expect a predictable result.

6. Real Estate Assistance

Many franchises offer assistance in obtaining leases and provide help negotiating with real estate brokers to get a good deal on the facility in which to build the business. Franchises realize that the facilities are one of the largest expenses that must be incurred and provide significant guidance to ensure this is a smooth and efficient process.

7. Construction Assistance

Franchisors tend to have built-out models and contractor guidelines that can provide substantial efficiencies when constructing properties. Very often they provide assistance in determining the layout including the amount of furniture versus open space. Unnecessary spending and uncertainty can be reduced when using the franchisor's models for construction.

8. Purchasing Power

This is one of the most crucial advantages to franchising. When franchises buy in bulk from all of their suppliers, their pricing per unit of various goods is substantially lower. This advantage can be significant. The leverage of a franchisor is much higher than that of an independent business.

9. Risk Aversion

This does not mean franchise ownership is a risk-free enterprise, but it does mean that many of the mistakes and common risks that new businesses make can be avoided. All business owners will make mistakes, especially new business owners, but those that choose the franchise route get history as their guide. Every lesson the franchisor teaches you from past experiences is one you will not have to learn through failure.

What might discourage franchising?

No matter how appealing this model sounds, one must be willing to analyze the multitude of challenges franchising entails. No system for running a company is perfect, and those people who work hard to overcome, minimize, and deal with the following challenges can succeed in this business. The following nine reasons can discourage franchising:

1. Profitability is not perfect

    Franchise owners must disclose earnings possibilities to their investors and provide a picture of the financial outlook, but one must realize that the profitability projections that are shown are usually the average profitability figures. There will be some entities that perform better or worse than the profitability projections. Plus, some franchisees incur different costs due to the location of their franchise. There can be different tax codes from county to county or state to state.

2. Start-Up Costs

    All franchises have some sort of start-up fee or cost structure. No business model is sold for free, so this cost must be accepted as a condition to owning a franchise and properly accounted for. A good metric for making sense of start up costs is to think about what you are getting from the franchisor. If you could accomplish the same thing yourself without the franchise, you should question the value that the franchisor provides.

3. Territorial Encroachment

    This is something franchise owners may deal with. Imagine you own a food franchise, and within six weeks of opening, another franchise from the same company opens a few blocks away. A portion of your previous clientele may be taken by this new location. Franchisors will typically grant some sort of exclusivity around a territory to prevent encroachment from happening.

4. Limited Independence

This means that no creative slogans can be used that are not approved by the parent company, and one can never decide to run the franchise their own way. Some franchisors provide more creative freedom than others; this must be kept in mind when exploring potential franchises.

5. Limited Legal Recourse

Depending on how franchisors and franchisees arrive at their agreements, there will always be limited legal rights for the franchisee. The franchisee can rarely sue the franchisor, and no matter how unfair the agreement may seem, options are limited. By becoming a franchisee, you are agreeing to a contract that the franchisor wrote. The contract will likely favor the writer.

6. Royalty Payments

There are payments that must be made to the franchisor, and the franchisor and franchisee must set up a fee structure. These royalties are most typically levied on gross revenues, not on profitability. The reason for this is simple; it is difficult for a franchisor to manage what expenses a franchisee claims as regular and legitimate, whereas gross revenue is a very simple number to evaluate.

7. Restriction on Post-Term Competition

If you decide that you do not wish to continue working with your franchisor, and you would like to start a similar company, you are likely out of luck. Almost all franchise agreements have non-compete clauses that stop you from creating similar businesses for a fixed amount of time once you terminate your relationship with the parent company.

8. Advertising Fees and Mandatory Upgrades

    There are sometimes fees beyond royalties that come into play in terms of advertising and upgrades. Franchisors have the ability to change their models if business conditions warrant it. Some franchisors also require upgrades of facilities and technology from time to time, and these are costs the franchisee must incur. These costs must be dealt with appropriately.

9. Termination

    Franchisors have the right to terminate the agreement and partnership under conditions that are spelled out in the franchise disclosure document. These are typically grouped into "curable" and "incurable" defaults. If a franchisor feels that you are running a business without following the model, doing anything that hurts the image of the franchise, or failing to adhere to the franchise agreement's terms, the franchisor has the right to ask you to "cure" the default. If you do not, the franchisor has the ability to terminate your agreement. There are other actions, such as committing a felony, filing for bankruptcy, or abandoning a business that are considered "incurable" defaults whereby the franchisor can terminate your agreement immediately.

Now we have examined franchises from the perspectives of both the franchisor and the franchisee. We have seen a multitude of reasons why a company may or may not franchise. We now understand why an individual chooses to own a franchise, and we have explored the challenges franchisees can experience.

Summary

The franchising of companies is a historic tradition that has been around for hundreds of years. With a franchise, you give up some of the positives of owning a business to reduce some of the negatives of owning a business. A franchisee buys the right to use the logo and image of the franchisor, as well as the company's business model. Like most things in life, owning a franchise has its perks and problems. Companies see it as a way to expand their reach, minimize risk, and create more value. Individuals look at it as a way to reduce their risk of failure and obtain a proven method with a track record for wealth creation while still running their own business. As a franchisee, it all comes down to understanding the risks, preparing for the risks, and researching every facet of the company. Follow the franchisors' methods if you choose to become a franchise, and do not sign any agreement until you have a thorough understanding of what you are signing. A prepared individual can take this business model to achieve his or her own success alongside the success of the franchisor.

According to the international franchise website, and with data collected by IHS Global Insight, the business index for franchise units has been less volatile than the S & P 500 for the past decade. The metrics used for this franchise index include but are not limited to franchise growth trends, consumption of certain goods and services, number of self-employed, and so on. The base years used for both index representations are January of 2000. It may be inferred from these indexes that franchised business as a whole generally have a more stable business growth in comparison to the aggregate of companies in the S & P 500.

Frachise Business Index

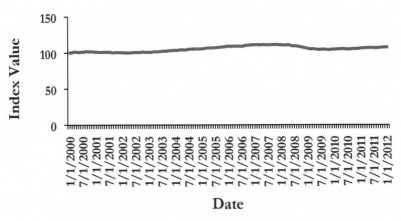

S & P Index

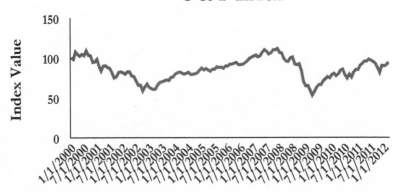

CHAPTER 7 - FINDING YOUR IDEAL FRANCHISE

Today, there are more than 2,600 franchise brands with more than 750,000 locations across the United States. The International Franchise Association (IFA) reports that franchises support nearly eighteen million jobs in America and account for $2.1 trillion of economic output for the U.S. economy. With all of these choices, it can be hard to find a franchise that is perfect for you. If you are diligent with your research, you can find the right franchise system. If you find the choices overwhelming, you can also retain a franchise consultant who will help you understand the options. It is crucial that you can answer the following two questions: Am I ready to be a franchise owner? Which franchise is right for me? Owning a franchise is like buying a business and getting married.

"Someone should not be attracted to franchising because it promises greater rewards. It is more about containing the risk. It is like getting married. You should be scouting for your partner, and this takes time."

—David Lewis, SPHR, VP of Express Employment Professionals

It is important to do your homework before investing. Franchises take a lot of the guesswork out of starting your own business. This does not mean that because the franchise brand is successful elsewhere that your specific location will be successful. So how do we find the perfect franchise? It is important to ask the right questions to make sure you will be satisfied. This list of ten questions should serve as a checklist as you are evaluating franchise options. Work your way down the list. If you answer yes to the next ten questions, you may be on the right path for professional and personal fulfillment.

1. Do I like the industry?

    You need to find a business that matches your interests and one that you can be passionate about. This motivates you to do well. Doing something you love is important for the new small business owner, especially in the beginning, as you may spend most of your waking hours at your business. If you are a vegan, a steak house may not be the right business to own. If you love caring for others and feel good from making those around you happy, you may want to consider an elder care business. Make sure that it is a business that you will enjoy running and is in an industry you can grow in. Just because you enjoy playing tennis does not mean that you will enjoy or be well suited to run a tennis supply franchise. Look for franchises in different industries. Kurt Landwehr, VP of Franchise Development at Regis Corp. (the largest hair salon franchise chain in the world), advises that when looking for an industry, evaluate the short and long term unseen effects. "Imagine fifteen years ago when people were lining up to get into the video business. Someone should have asked, "How could changing technology impact on this model." While it is important to consider the goods and services of the franchise, this should not be the deciding factor of the franchise that you chose.

2. Does the franchise have a good reputation?

    It is important to make sure the company is in good standing or unknown within the local community where you plan to open a location. It is far better to purchase a franchise that is not known and create the reputation than to purchase one that has a bad reputation that causes consumers to avoid you. If it is a well-known franchise, call five people and ask them for their opinion of this brand. Ask them if, as a customer, they would purchase a product or service from this brand. Red flags that would show up in the FDD are if the franchise has pending lawsuits against it or a history of litigation with its franchisees.

3. Are the other franchisees within your franchise of choice satisfied?

    Again, do not be afraid to reach out people. Take some time to speak with other franchisees. Call five franchisees and ask them the following questions:

    - Are you happy with the overall culture of the company?
    - Do you receive the support you need from the franchisor?
    - Would you do this again?

    Also, it is important to consider contacting people who were previously franchisees within the company to get their viewpoints. One resource to consider is the Franchise Research Institute (www.franchiseresearchinstitute.com). This institute conducts a degree of due diligence, providing tools such as a review of the company's FDD and license contracts. This is included in the FRI research report. These reports provide independent assessment of franchisee's enthusiasm towards their franchisors. By sampling all franchisees in a specific area that have owned the franchise for seven years or less, FRI seeks an unbiased assessment of the franchisor. Of course, you must do your own research to verify for yourself any data that you come across.

4. Where will you open the franchise?

Location. Location. Location. This is the mantra of buying properties, owning businesses, and even picking parking spaces. This can be one of the most critical business decisions, especially when opening a business that depends on foot traffic. Just because a business thrives in one area does not mean it will in another area. Franchisors will often require certain location specifications, such as traffic flow and accessibility.

Here is a simple test to get a sense of traffic going past a given location. Take a people counter or a pad of paper and sit at a business or in a car next to your target location. Go at various times and count how many people walk past within fifteen minutes. This test allows you to see how overall traffic will be and when the best times to do business are. Make sure the franchise you are looking at has a good team of professionals to help advise you on how to grow your business.

5. Is the franchise well known in the local area?

Your favorite childhood franchise from your hometown may not be as popular as you think in your current location. While there may be adequate foot traffic, you may need to convince your local community that you offer high-quality product just like the more well-known brands in the area. Buying into the iconic brands with their well known logos may be more expensive initially, but it can save you long term marketing costs and require less legwork to bring in customers.

6. Do you have the finances for buying into the franchise?

    The more successful the franchise, the more well known the brand will be; buying into such a franchise can be very expensive. Dana Mead, Director of Franchise Development at Kahala Franchising (one of the largest franchisors of quick serve restaurants in the US), advises that while there might be a high average unit volume (AUV) in stores, when you boil down your revenues after expenses, you may not reach your expected profit. Having realistic expectations is very important. She also shares three key insights:

    1. As previously discussed, location is a major piece of the puzzle.
    2. Deliver the experience in the store that keeps people coming back. If you do not deliver the experience, the customers will walk right by your store.
    3. Franchisors need to supply marketing on a franchise concept level, whether a small or national brand. This is spelled out in the FDD.

7. Will the franchise provide assistance in business dealings?

    What are the support mechanisms that the franchisor has to support you as the franchisee? Many franchisors understand that you are a new business owner and will offer their franchisees assistance. Just like you do not want to fail, neither do the franchisors. Failure promotes a bad image about the brand and benefits neither business owner nor franchisor.

    You know what you are good at, having already crossed the first rock of this book. It is nearly impossible for you as a business owner to be able to execute your business on your own. Focus on those tasks you are best suited for, and ask for assistance in the areas where you are lacking.

    With any business, marketing is important in order to spread the word and get customers into your business.

Franchisors often allocate funds specifically for marketing. They understand that everyone has a different skill set. For example, if you are an expert in bookkeeping and can manage your books, but you are a little shy and not as strong at making sales, it is important to ask if the company offers assistance to help you develop your sales and presentation skills. Find franchisors that offer comprehensive initial and continuing education training courses for the benefit of their franchisees. Like any world-class company, a quality franchisor is going to invest heavily into their support mechanisms. Every franchisor I have ever spoken with about the quality of their support has waxed poetic about their support department, even if that consisted of one teenager in a cubicle. It is your job to understand exactly what is meant by support and then verify that it really exists. It is important to understand to what level a franchisor will have oversight over your business. Some franchisees chafe at the franchisor when they micromanage their business. "I didn't buy a franchise to have *'big brother'* looking over my shoulder" is a refrain I have heard in the past. Do you want a hands-on company that will give you strict guidelines, or do you want the freedom to run your own business? While it is important to have a franchisor that will help you manage your business, understand how heavy the franchisor's influence is. This is a personal preference for each business owner.

8. Are you as a new owner allowed to make decisions for the business that you feel add value?

A good franchisee is someone who loves what the franchisor has... someone who is an enthusiast... who does not go to try and change the franchise model.

—Rhonda Sanderson, Owner of Sanderson & Associates

Franchisors specify which products or services the franchise will offer. This structure and control can be comforting for first-time business owners who want to be shown the ropes. Some franchisors permit their franchisees to add to their inventory and add to the goods and services that it provides. This is also a personal preference for many new business owners. Some are more comfortable using the established protocol while others want the freedom to adapt as they see fit. This is something you should also ask about when you call five franchisees. Make sure that the franchisor's management style aligns with your personal preferences.

Micromager **Management Continuum** No Manager

9. Does the franchisor provide employee training for its franchisees?

Large franchisors will often have their own training center and require mandatory franchise training for the franchisee's staff. This allows for consistent delivery of service, which is important for franchises that have several locations. For those that do not have such programs, it is left up to the franchise owner to create his or her own training program for staff.

10. Can I devote the necessary time to this franchise?

There is a wide spectrum of franchise owners. There are those who can spend every waking moment at the business and those who have to balance work and family. Ask yourself how much of your day you can commit to opening and operating a franchise, and find a franchise that aligns with your schedule and commitments. Call five franchise owners and ask them how they balance their time. In speaking with these franchisees, you will have a better understanding of both checklist items nine and ten for the franchise you are looking to invest in.

Four-Step Process For Calling Franchisors and Franchisees

1. *Share*
2. *Interact*
3. *Engage*
4. *Ask*

—Paul Segreto, CEO of Franchise Foundry

Finding the perfect franchise is possible if you put the effort in when researching franchises and reflecting on your personal preferences. Most importantly, keep an open mind while searching. Pick a business model that aligns with your skill set. Do not make it an emotionally driven decision—look for a good fit to your lifestyle.

Once you have made your phone calls and narrowed it down to a few franchises, it is time for Discovery Day (or D-Day). This might be the first face-to-face meeting you have with the franchisors you have chosen. Discovery Day offers the opportunity for you to meet the corporate workers and visit a local franchisee.

D-Day is when you walk into the front door at our corporate headquarters and there are seventy-five people there waiting to greet you. Everyone here is to support you, to train you.

People feel comfortable in joining a system with the team in their corner. I don't want to enter into a ten- year agreement with someone unless we can all look into each other's eyes.

—Alex Roberts, CFE, President at Mr. Handyman International, LLC

The time you have spent in investigating your franchise is one of the most important investments you can make in your future as a franchisee.

CHAPTER 8 - TYPES OF FRANCHISE MODELS AND LICENSE STRUCTURES

This chapter is intended to clarify the different types of franchises and franchisees. A common misconception is that franchises are only for small-business owners. You can also build a business empire through a franchise if this is your goal. First, it is important to talk about what type of franchisee you want to be. Many franchise owners go out and buy a franchise based on what its product or service is. Unsuccessful franchise experiences often stem from an individual's affinity to a product rather than an understanding of the underlying fundamentals of a business and how they relate to that individual's skill sets and abilities. If you are good in the kitchen, and you love food, you may want to own a restaurant. This very often leads to failure, as success in owning a restaurant is not about being a great chef, it's really about successfully running a business.

Let me introduce you to the Golden Rule shared by Doug Schadle, CEO of Rhino 7 Development: "Figure out how much money you have to invest." The easiest way to own a multi-million dollar operation is to buy one; however, this option exists for a small group of people who have the capital needed to buy an already successful operation. Also, they run the danger of not having the expertise required to maintain the success of the business. There are a myriad of franchised business out there but, structurally, most franchises fall into these three categories; "owner-operator," "executive," or "semi-absentee executive" model of business. The easiest metric to evaluate these by in relation to your situation is to think through what you have more of; time or money? If you have more money than time, you have the ability to be in more of an "absentee" or "semi-absentee" owner role since you can deploy your capital to hire employees. If you have less money and more time, then you are going to be the employee and you should look at more of an "owner-operator" type business.

Three Models of Franchise Businesses

Owner-Operator Model

In this model, the owner implements the business. The owner works full time in the business, managing and delivering the products and services to the customer. As the owner implements the business, he or she makes all of the profit after franchise fees and expenses. If you were interested in buying a carpet-cleaning franchise, the franchisor will train you and show you how to advertise your business, and then you would go to work cleaning carpets. This type of franchise requires the least investment and can achieve sales rapidly, but the gains tend to be modest. The owner- operator franchises are typically buying a job and looking to replace their income. To build a really big owner-operator business, you will need to start with a concept that has the potential to grow a single operation to a multi-million dollar level. However, once you grow an operation to that level, you will need to add layers of management, which results in the executive model.

Executive Model

In the executive model, the owner hires a team to manage

everything from sales to maintenance to delivery of the goods and services. This allows him or her to expand the operation but requires significant investment in the labor of others. By managing a full team, you have higher earning potential and larger income. The advantage of the owner-operator model is that it is usually easier for you to be personally invested in the business, but this limits growth to the amount that you can personally produce. This limitation is not present in the executive model, but the executive model requires more capital to grow a big business. If you have the capital, growing a big business through the executive model can occur much more rapidly. There is usually a tradeoff between the first two strategies; however, building a significant enterprise is possible with both in the long term. The decision comes down to a question of committing time versus money.

Semi-Absentee/Absentee Executive Model

In the semi-absentee/absentee model, the owner builds a number of units that operate independently of each other to deliver the products and services to the customer. The key is building a team whereby different people report to you, the owner, and you manage each franchise unit through a manager. You as the owner do not directly manage the team. Instead you manage a team of managers who run the facilities. These owners are developers who expand their operations to more units. This type of franchise is more capital intensive than other types of franchises.

The supreme way to make money from the franchise system is to buy three or more of a strong concept. I worked at Subway when they were a very young system. Those franchisees that owned three, four, or five franchises cashed out as multi-millionaires. Multiples are the way to go.

—Rhonda Sanderson, Owner of Sanderson & Associates

In order to start figuring out which model is best for you, figure out how much capital you have to work with and how much you need to support the kind of lifestyle you need. How long of a time frame are you willing to allow for the business to be built? Now you have the different methods to achieve your ideals of success. If you want to commit less capital and own a franchise that you can be personally invested in with faster returns, the owner-operator model is best. This requires you to be 100 percent committed to your business, as you are on call 24/7. If there is something that the business needs, goods that need to be sold, and services that need to be provided, you are responsible. This can be both comforting from a control point of view and occasionally overwhelming, since you are both the head cook and bottle washer.

There are lots of great franchise businesses that can be used as the foundations for building successful empires. If this is your goal, the secret is to finding the right type of business for you, the right type of franchise. In my opinion, there are four types of franchises that you can buy into. These are:

- Simple Retail
- Sophisticated Retail
- Service to Business (B2B)
- Service to Consumer (B2C)

Simple Retail
Consumer Only – Totally Reactive

Simple retail franchises are those that you would typically find in a small strip center. These are the types of businesses that do not have significant scale in operations, or in other words, they do not have very large operations. Simple retail franchises start with you standing behind a counter providing a product or service that people demand. This type of cash-and-carry business is easy to build and attracts consumers, but the earnings are limited. There are plenty of other options and alternatives. Sales are key to this type of businesses.

Examples: Food, Tax Prep, Fitness

Sophisticated Retail
Inventory and Somewhat Reactive/ Proactive Marketing

Sophisticated retail franchises take simple retail and scale them to larger shopping centers. These are bigger businesses with a different approach to sales. Rather than one a customer arriving at your store knowing what to purchase, the consumers or businesses come to seek your expertise before making their purchase. This type of franchise requires more than just high sales to succeed. One needs marketing, referrals, advertisements, and direct mailing solicitation to attract new business. This type of business will require you to manage a staff to run the place.

Examples: Sign Shop, Printing Shop, Urgent Care, Auto Repair

Service to Business
Very Proactive Marketing

A service-to-business franchise provides services that businesses need. Think of the old adage "Have your back office be someone else's front office." You are providing the services that a business finds are more efficient and cost effective to outsource. This type of franchise usually requires you to travel to the customer's location and give an estimate before closing a deal. The service and product is delivered and sold directly to clients at their businesses. This franchise model requires the most marketing with cold calls, networking, and advertising.

Examples: Commercial Cleaning, Drug Testing, Business Coaching, Employment Services

Service to Consumer
Proactive Marketing

Service-to-consumer franchises are similar to service-to-business franchises except that the services are delivered to a client's home or you are providing a service to individuals. This business similarly requires proactive marketing.

Examples: Painting, Senior Care, Pest Control Services, Property Services, Childcare

Just as you analyze the types of businesses that are available and your relationships with customers and employers, you should analyze the industries. Bold entrepreneurs who think the possibilities of high rewards are worth the high risk develop new industries. While this may seem lucrative, it is the job of these business owners to educate consumers on a need and then sell them their solution. Still, many franchisors thrive in proven industries with a shortage of providers. Succeeding as a franchisee is all about realizing and taking advantage of the current situation.

Franchising overall is more varied than most people are aware with different structures, types of businesses, and price levels. Even within a type of franchise business, there are three models of obtaining a franchise license, and it is crucial to explore each. These models include master license, regional developer, and unit franchisor.

Types of Franchise License:

Single-Unit License

A single-unit franchisee buys the right to operate a single franchise unit. Typically, most franchisees will start off as a single-unit franchise. This allows you to learn about franchising with the minimum investment before you consider additional units. The single-unit franchisee may have a small radius of exclusive territory to operate within; typically this may be a two-or three-mile radius around the store, a collection of zip codes or some sort of geographic qualifiers. The single-unit franchisee is heavily involved in all of the operations of the business.

Regional Developer License

The regional developer franchise license grants the franchisee the right to open a number of franchises in a given area. The franchisor usually determines the schedule for when the franchisee has to open a number of franchises in the territory. If the franchisee adheres to the schedule, then he or she has exclusive rights to franchise in that area. Area development franchisees may also have the benefit of paying reduced franchise and royalty fees on a per unit basis. The territories range from a town to parts of or all of a city. In order to find optimal locations, the franchisor will typically have their own real estate department or work with a qualified real estate broker. Having to manage all of the locations, the area development franchisee will require help to manage the units.

Master License

A master license franchisee assumes a larger area than the regional developer, but in addition to opening their own franchised locations, master license franchisees can also sell single-unit and regional development licenses, yielding additional profits from these sales. The master franchisee will receive a part of the royalties paid by each contracted franchisee. The master franchisee will operate at least one unit for income purposes and for training contracted franchisees. Master franchise licenses tend to be expensive but can have a high potential return on investment. The territory associated can be a large area, a state, or even a country. Similarly to the regional developer, as long as the master franchisee adheres to the schedule, they will be able to have exclusive rights to develop the business. The skill sets required to be successful are significant, as you are, in essence, becoming a franchisor yourself.

As you explore options, make sure you keep sight of what your current situation is. Know how much time and capital you have to commit, and then find the model that aligns with your abilities. Once you have decided on the model and license type, you can select the franchise that is right for you.

CHAPTER 9 - TARGETING FRANCHISORS TO INVESTIGATE

This chapter is designed to empower you with the tools and resources to find a franchisor that is right for you.

The number one franchise resource that is available to both prospective and veteran franchisees is the International Franchise Association Web site, www.franchise.org. The IFA is the world's oldest and largest organization representing the franchising sector. There are over 2,600 franchised brands representing almost 750,000 locations. Each year, the IFA puts out a very interesting white paper entitled "The Franchise Business Economic Outlook" it's a good read and one I highly recommend. IFA was founded with the purpose of protecting, enhancing, and promoting franchising. Bill Rosenberg, the founder of the IFA in 1959, explained the importance of the IFA as follows:

When people got hurt and lost their money in a franchise arrangement, the first thing they did was complain to their congressman or state legislator. These guys, not knowing anything about franchising or having any credible source of information, wanted to pass laws that would make it difficult to survive as a franchisor. The goal of IFA was to educate the public and the lawmakers.

— Bill Rosenberg, Founder of the IFA

The IFA currently estimates there are over 2,600 franchise opportunities representing seventy-five industries, covering everything from auto repair to wine bars. With so many choices, you can find the right franchise opportunity. The first step is to pick a few industries that you would enjoy and feel provide good opportunities. This requires you to do some soul searching of what industries you want to operate in. If the industry that you are working in is your forte, but you are tired for working for someone else, perhaps it is time to find a franchise in the same or similar industry. If not, then it is time to find something new. Whatever you decide, search for a franchise that excites you but keep your feet firmly planted on the ground; this will allow you to grow with your business. When you are looking into franchising, search engines are probably your first line of attack. There is, of course, a multitude of websites concerning franchised business. Here are a few:

Franchising Web sites:

- Franchise.org
- Entreprenur.org
- Franchiseopportunities.com
- Franchisesolutions.com
- Franchise.com
- Franchiseworks.com
- Franchisesolutions.com
- Franchiseforsale.com

The IFA Web site in particular, franchise.org, provides a list of franchise opportunities in each industry with a brief description and a link to their home pages. This will help you find hundreds of opportunities to help you find the right business. Like looking at the stock market, you can find a huge list of stocks that you can go through and research yourself, or you can go through printed resources to see the latest recommendations. This research can help you understand the landscape before you dive in to investigate. Magazines and newspapers are also a great resource. Here are some of my favorites:

- *Entrepreneur Magazine*
- *INC Magazine*
- *QSR Magazine*
- *Successful Franchising Magazine*
- *USA Today* (Thursday's edition)
- *Wall Street Journal* (Thursday's edition)

Also, if you are looking for information from the government, the U.S. Small Business Administration's Small Business Development Center is a fantastic resource: www.sbaonline.sba.gov/sbdc.

Once you get a general sense of what you are interested in and what are good opportunities, you are ready to go out and meet your prospective franchisor. Trade shows and expositions allow you to "speed date" the franchisors that you are interested in to find out if they are right for you. In the spring, the IFA sponsors the International Franchise Expo, one of the world's largest gathering of franchise companies. At this venue, over twenty thousand attendees typically come to meet hundreds of franchisors. There are also a multitude of smaller franchise shows that occur around the country and are open to the public. The IFA also sponsors several trade shows year round and there are multiple franchise trade shows that happen around the country. This is not only a great opportunity to find a business but also to gain knowledge as you begin the processes of owning your own franchise. They provide excellent educational materials and a great breadth of people that you can keep in contact with to build relationships and learn from. As you travel to these trade shows, you can find interesting businesses that are not in your community. Keep an open mind, and keep your eyes and ears open. Opportunities are everywhere.

Franchise Consultant:

For additional skilled advice, a good option to consider is a franchise consultant. There are many names for this segment of business brokerage, such as "franchise broker" or "franchise coach." Sometimes, superlatives such as "senior franchise consultant," "regional vice-president," "principal," or "owner" are added to their titles. These usually do not have much merit other than in the mind of the bestower. I have never seen a "junior franchise consultant" title, but that may exist somewhere. Each industry has experts, and there is always a range of quality that you can find in any industry.

Know what they call someone who graduated dead last in his or her medical class with the lowest GPA? Doctor. The same goes for the person who graduated first in his or her class. It is the same in any profession. An experienced franchise consultant can answer your questions and guide you through the selection process. Typically, an experienced consultant is going to have relationships with a large number of franchisors and know the key executives on a personal basis. This can be a tremendous asset to you as you will be introduced to decision makers at a franchise system. This tends to engender more of a partnership orientation on both the franchisor and the prospective franchisee. Just like you are using this book to help guide you through this journey, a franchise consultant can provide you with the support system that you need to help you find the business model that is right for you. Franchise consultants will also help you define the dreams that you hope to accomplish by determining your ideal level of franchise ownership. Consultants will determine your skills and match them with companies that you will thrive at. This will save you time and effort, helping you focus on a few top-quality firms.

The Three Essential Traits of a Great Franchise Consultant:

- Level of Franchise Experience

    The more your consultant knows, the better job he or she will do in finding you the perfect franchise. Look for a consultant who has worked in franchising on many different levels, one who has had experience with franchisor's executive teams.

- Reputation in the Industry

    Reputation is everything. A reputable consultant will do what is best for you, the prospective franchisee, to achieve your goals and vision.

- Proven Results

    At the end of the day, you do not just want a franchise consultant who will hold your hand through the entire process and tell only what you want to hear. You want someone who is going to challenge you to make certain that you know what you are doing. You want someone who will help you deliver results, and this is the easiest of the three traits to assess. The franchise consultant will work with reputable franchisors and know about the traits that make franchisees successful within each system. When you do well, the consultant does well.

A quality franchise consultant is an experienced business person with significant business credentials. With the multitude of professional Web sites, such as LinkedIn, you are able to get a quick understanding of your consultant's background to see if you are comfortable with their professional and educational credentials. With the wide range of consultants out there, you can find ones who are local to your market and will want to meet you face to face, or even offer to come to your home to visit. There are others who will recommend multiple companies on the first phone call without knowing who you are or what is important to you. The range of credentials and experience you can encounter is vast. There are consultants who have no experience in franchising and consultants who have just purchased a franchise to be a consultant. You can also find consultants who were executives in significant franchise companies and are well known and regarded in the industry. Do your homework and actively interview your consultant prior to engaging their services to ensure that his or her credentials and experience are a good fit for your expectations. This will help you ensure that you are not someone's test subject as he or she is learning a new career!

Here is a helpful checklist to go through when picking an advisor, whether legal, financial, or business-related:

1. How much experience does that advisor have in franchising?
2. What is your advisor's educational background?
3. What is the average income and expertise of your advisor's clientele? Does this match your expectations?
4. Does this advisor have experience that aligns with your requirements?
5. Does your advisor have significant professional credentials?
6. How is your advisor compensated?
7. What is the advisor's interest in helping you achieve your dream?
8. What is the responsibility of the advisor?
9. What is your advisor's typical method of contact with clients? Is it proactive or reactive? Does this work well with your preferences?
10. Do you trust your advisor?
11. Does this advisor fill your needs to achieve your goals?
12. Does your advisor actively seek to educate you?
13. Is the advisor part of a larger organization that provides a tested strategy to help him or her achieve your goals?
14. Do you like this person?

A franchise consultant will provide you with valuable services and will be honest with his or her assessment. If the consultant thinks you are ready to be a franchisee, he or she can work with you to create a framework to understand business ownership. If the consultant does not think you are ready, you should expect a direct and honest assessment; this can save you significant loss later on. What are your obligations? Time. Most franchise consultants offer their services to their clients free of charge. If and when you decide to choose a franchisor, the broker then receives compensation by the franchisor. This is similar to the compensation model of an executive recruiter or a realtor and ensures the consultant's interest is aligned with yours. If you do not find the right franchise, or the franchisor does not award you a franchise, they are not compensated.

When considering working with a franchise advisor, my recommendation is to always think about the values that your prospective advisor is exhibiting through their actions. Honesty better be the first one. As Thoreau said "Rather than love, than money, than fame, give me truth". The truth is what you are looking for in your franchise investigation and you want to surround yourself with people who are not afraid to tell it.

Values are our fundamental beliefs. They are the principles we use to define what is right, good and just. Values provide guidance as we determine right versus wrong and good versus bad. They are our standards.

Consider the word "evaluate". It literally means, that which we place "value" upon or to fix the worth of something. When we evaluate something we compare it to a standard. We determine whether it meets that standard or falls short, comes close or far exceeds. To evaluate is to determine the merit of an action. When investigating a franchise or a franchise advisor be certain to evaluate every aspect of that business and the person who is recommending these businesses to you.

Typical values include honesty, integrity, compassion, courage, honor, responsibility, patriotism, respect and fairness.

Great companies and individuals we universally respect understand what values should never change and what can be changed. This ability to practice continuity and change simultaneously is often predicated upon a discipline to anchor a few core values. These core values define the very existence of an entity even if it means that sometimes their adherence to these values create a competitive *dis*-advantage.

Working with a reputable franchise consultant can get you connected with quality franchisors. Quality in every aspect of life is paramount. Certainly, through your ownership of a quality franchise, this will help you pave the way for success as a franchisee. In the final analysis, this means running a sustainable and profitable business, building a base of satisfied customers, and building long term brand equity.

CHAPTER 10 - COMMUNICATION WITH FRANCHISORS

Owning a franchise is not *buying* a franchise. It is not the same type of transaction. It is creating a partnership where you and the franchisor both want certain things and are willing to give up certain things to achieve this. Oftentimes, however, I have seen cynicism creep into the process and destroy the relationship between the franchisor and franchisee before it can begin. This chapter will give you an understanding of what a franchisor is looking for in a prospective partner.

As you start finding franchise options that interest you, the next logical step is to speak with the franchisors. There will be a qualification process on both sides. You are looking to understand what the franchisor brings to the table and if your abilities coupled with the franchisors system bring you the kind of lifestyle and income you require. The franchisors are interested in knowing if you are the right fit for their systems as well. It is a delicate balance that is part business and part personal.

Your first communication with a franchisor is likely to be with a franchise salesperson (also known as a franchise developer) who reports to the vice president of development. The vice president typically reports to the CEO of the company. You can tell a lot about a franchise by the quality of the first interaction. Does it seem professional? Is it an organized conversation? Does it feel like an interview? It should. It is.

Top franchise systems employ professionals who can sell and also have the ability to connect what makes their system successful with the competencies of the person on the other end of the line. Low-end franchise systems are going to be about selling you a franchise at all costs. The quality franchise developers are going to talk about the realities of owning a franchise and then ask you questions about your background to understand if you have the traits that make successful owners.

Owning a franchise is a big commitment to a partnership. Both the franchisor and franchisee have to be willing participants, and the best partnerships tend to have a foundation that is based on transparency and trust. Just as you are looking to become part of a franchise system, the franchisor is looking at you trying to figure out if you are the right person for their company. If you are married or in a significant relationship, think of the steps that it took to get you to where you are now. If you have been through a divorce or a break-up, think of some of the early warning signs that you may have neglected to pay attention to that lead to the break up. Apply the knowledge you garnered from building your personal relationships when deciding whether to enter into a franchise business relationship.

Owning a franchise is like a marriage. I think this is the most powerful analogy to remind yourself of when looking at a franchise company. This is not a platitude. The franchisor is not doing this because the franchisor likes the way you look or your educational background seems impressive. Let us look at the cold-hearted capitalistic reason for this. The franchisor is going to make their money by levying a royalty on your gross revenues. This is their income. If they award the franchise to the wrong person, they are now married to that person, and it could be a long time before they can collect any meaningful royalty. Since franchisors are selling a territory-based business, once the territory is gone, they cannot put someone else into the territory. When you own a franchise, you and the franchisor are contractually bound for a period of time, usually ten years.

The worst thing that can happen to a franchisor is:

1. The franchisor awards the franchise to the wrong person
2. That person consumes a huge amount of the franchisor's resources for training and support
3. That person's business never grows and limps along, draining resources from the franchisor without paying the franchisor a meaningful royalty
4. A more qualified person comes along later but cannot be a part of the system because the territory is sold

The stakes for attracting and nurturing top performers in a franchise system are significant. Top performers in a franchise system, like in any organization, tend to account for the greatest contribution to the bottom line. They motivate other franchisees within the system. They are leaders and contributors to the growth of the overall system. They are the franchisor's most valuable assets. They are the ones whose royalties subsidize the low-performing franchisees in the system, pay the salaries of the franchisor's staff, and dream up new ways of gaining market share.

Conversely, low-performing franchisees can decimate a system. Low-quality franchisors will often point to a failing franchisee and say that they did not follow the system. Sometimes that is legitimately true, but if that is the story for every failing franchise, perhaps the question to ask the franchisor is "Why did they neglect to follow the system?" or "Why did you sell that person a franchise if you felt that person would not follow the system?" Failing franchisees not only incur a tremendous cost to themselves but also to the brand and their fellow franchisees.

Both the franchisee and the franchisor can derive value from the arrangement only if the franchise succeeds, otherwise the franchisor should do a strategic buyback and change that franchised business into an operating business.

—Tom Seeger, N'Hance Franchise Owner

When looking at quality franchise systems, one of the biggest mistakes I see first-time prospective franchisees fall into is thinking that they are buying a franchise and assuming the attitude of a buyer who needs to be sold. They are not *buying* a business. They are being *awarded* a franchise and should assume the attitude of creating a partnership. There is a big difference between the two. Usually, the attitude of "being sold" comes because the prospective candidate has no experience in creating a business partnership or had experience with franchisors who were desperately and aggressively trying to sell them a franchise. Just as there are quality franchise companies out there, there are also low-quality franchise companies. The hallmark of a low-quality system is that the franchisor is trying to sell you a franchise because the franchisor needs to add a unit. Selling you a franchise is how they make their money. This is typical of the franchise czar that we described earlier. We want to stay away from this type of franchisor.

Challenges occur when the prospective franchisee, having previously experienced this kind of selling situation, starts to put up walls and begins to shop for a franchise. Think of how you react when you walk into a store, pick up some merchandise, and a salesman walks up and says, "Can I help you?" The typical response is "I am just looking." Now put that into a dating situation. Think back to when you met your spouse or significant other. Is that the way the relationship started? Imagine how your partner would have felt if you treated them that way. Nonetheless, I see this kind of behavior consistently from people who are looking to own a franchise.

Consumer behavior has changed dramatically over the years. If you understand the reasons behind your actions as a consumer, you will become empowered to evaluate how you are acting when you are talking with franchisors and put yourself into a position to better increase your odds of achieving a meaningful partnership.

Over the years, as choices have become more abundant and the volume of purchases made by individuals has increased, the fear of making the wrong choice has also increased. This hyper-consumerism has created disconnectedness in consumers, as the more they own, the more empty they feel. Perhaps you know the term "retail therapy," where you purchase something, and it makes you feel good for a period of time. Owning a franchise can feel the same way, with an initial burst of happiness coming from owning a business and achieving independence. However, we need to be careful that we are evaluating the underlying business and not attribute the feelings of potential independence to the act of owning the franchise.

Consumers have less and less trust in the institutions that are selling them products. Think of the proliferation of sites like Angie's List or other peer-generated reviews. Most people are more willing to believe something that consumers have said about a product than what the manufacturer says, and for good reason—the manufacturer has a vested interest in selling the product.

Booz & Company, a global strategy firm established in 1914, defined the dominant mentality in U.S. consumers in a study as "the new frugality." This mentality is characterized by a strong awareness of the value that dictates compromises in terms of price, brand, and comfort. These are important attributes to consider when looking at franchised business as an owner but also in looking at their offerings through the eyes of a consumer. Does the franchise product or services fit these criteria? Are they something that there is a need for?

In addition to this strong awareness of value, there is another dynamic at play: the willingness to walk away. When evaluating significant expenditure items, most consumers tend to have a fallback or a logical replacement if one brand is not fulfilling their needs. This is easy when it comes to buying a car; it is significantly harder when evaluating franchises, as potential franchisees must often evaluate multiple brands across multiple industries. Walking away from a franchise investigation at the first whiff of an issue may be the right thing to do, or it may be throwing the baby out with the bath water.

There are few acquisitions that are as fraught with emotion as choosing a franchise. There is significant anxiety around making the wrong choice. The consequences of this anxiety are reticence to make decisions and risk avoidance. Some of the symptoms are the need for more and more information. However, at some point, you will encounter information overload. You cannot make a decision based solely upon an abundance of information. Analysis paralysis sets in, and the ability to make a decision is decimated. At some point, you have to make a yes-or-no decision. That is the hardest part for most people; hence the buying behaviors that creep into your investigation that will negatively impact that decision. Think of this as active pessimism. You are entering into the investigation with a mindset that is potentially destructive to your ability to make a clear decision.

Imagine your first date with someone. Imagine going into it with the idea that your date was going to try and convince you to do something that you did not want to do. Your guard would be up. The date would probably be the last, and even if it turned into a relationship, it would likely fail.

What are franchisors looking for?

I have always found the key to a successful partnership can be summed up with the acronym "SKI"

- Skill
- Knowledge
- Interest

Of these, the most important by far is interest. If you have the interest to do something, you will find a way to do it. It is always easier if the skill and the knowledge are congruent to the task at hand, and this is typically what the franchisor is trying to ascertain.

Keeping the dating and marriage analogy in mind, think of what a quality franchisor is going to appreciate. There are the tactical, nuts-and-bolts parts of a relationship that show courtesy. Show up on time, be prepared, be nice, be interested, and be engaged. It is amazing how far a little common sense will go.

A franchisor is going to be interested in understanding, at the beginning, the answers to questions in the following categories:

1. Fit

   Are you a fit for this system? Are your professional background and abilities going to give you the necessary foundation for success in their system?

2. Need

   Why do you want a franchise at this juncture in your life? What life purpose are you trying to achieve through acquisition of this franchise? Is it a good reason? Is it a reason that will strengthen you and guide you while you undertake the task of building a business?

3. Time Frame

   When do you want to do this? When do you want to start? When do you want your business open? Just because you might be a good fit does not mean you will be awarded a franchise, especially if your time frame does not match up with that of the franchisor. If you are looking to make a decision in one year, the likely response you will get from a franchisor is "Call me in nine months." The response from a low-end franchisor will be to convince you to change your time frame.

4. Money

   Are you sufficiently capitalized to allow you to actually purchase this franchise and capitalize it through the necessary period of time that the franchisor knows to be important to get the business established and cash flowing? The number one reason businesses fail is that the owner runs out of money. If all you have is enough for the franchise fee, do not do it! It is like buying a car because you are planning on a cross-country trip and not having enough money for gas. You are not going to get far. Beware of the franchisor who makes special deals with you or tries to convince you that your lack of capitalization can be overcome along the way. These franchisors are just trying to take your money.

5. Decision Makers

Who is going to own this business? Who has the responsibility for making the decisions? If you are married or have a significant other, they need to be on board. The franchisor does not want to spend significant time and resources on working with you only to hear "My wife does not want to do this." Would you really want to do something if your spouse or significant other was not fully supportive?

Structuring the Conversations with the Franchisor

Great franchise systems hire great franchise developers to help them find great franchisees. In my experience, great franchise developers tend to be inquisitive. They want to know about you. That is their job. The old adage, "we have two ears and one mouth so that we can listen twice as much as we speak" is important. Great developers ask questions that are relevant and give them a deeper understanding of who you are and what you are trying to accomplish. Low-end salespeople tend to talk and talk and talk.

Conversations with franchisors should follow a fairly logical progression. It is during the first calls that we form our most important opinions, and our antennae need to be up as to the quality of franchisor. You should be asking as many questions about the franchise salesperson as they are of you. What is their background? What does the salesperson think of the economy? What has the salesperson seen as the key attributes of success in the system? Does the salesperson like his or her job? These answers all should be reasonable and intelligent. The salesperson should have a significant history in franchising and business. If not, you should question the quality of the company, especially if the face (or voice) of the company— the first interaction that a prospective franchisee has with the company—is a low-end affair.

The first part of the conversation is going to be about you. Quality franchisors will usually have you fill out an application and send in a resume prior to the first call so they can prepare. Expect to get a wide range of questions that touch upon the following:

1. Career
2. Family
3. Financial History

Typical questions include:

1. What is your plan?
2. Why do you need a franchise?
3. What are your family & friends saying?
4. Where will the funding come from?
5. Why partner with a franchise?
6. What do you hope to accomplish?
7. What keeps you up at night?
8. What is your work history?
9. What do you currently do?
10. What are your responsibilities?
11. Why are you looking to start a business?
12. What are you looking for a business to produce?
13. What would you like to be earning one, three, and five years out?
14. What is your educational background?
15. What kind of money does it take to cover your household expenses?
16. Are you married? Do you have kids? How old are they?
17. Do you have significant expenses, such as college, on the horizon?
18. Do you have a family budget?
19. Do you track your finances?

Personal questions that would not be acceptable or legal in a traditional job interview are commonly asked. Quality franchisors are going to want to understand your family dynamic and how an investment in a business is going to impact that. If your family is not on board with this decision, it is likely going to cause you significant distress, which is going to distract you from building a business.

Answer openly and transparently. There is nothing to be gained by lying or by getting offended by the questions (unless the question is way off base). This conversation is about two people looking to create a partnership.

Your turn

Questions that are okay to ask the franchisor:

1. What is the mission or the values of your company?
2. What is the history of your franchise company?
   a. When did the company start?
   b. How many units are open?
   c. How many units are slated for development?
   d. Are there development plans in my area?
   e. What are the company's long-term objectives?
   f. If there are failed units, how many, and why did they fail?
3. Concept
   a. What are the company's products?
   b. How is the company unique?
   c. What need does the company fill in the market?
   d. How it is priced?
   e. How many employees are necessary?
   f. How it the concept promoted?
   g. Who is the competition?
   h. How does this franchisor differentiate its products or services from the competition's offerings?
4. Industry
   a. What is the size of the industry?

    b. What are the other relevant industry data?

    c. What is the Standard Industrial Classification "SIC" or North American Industry Classification System "NAICS" Code for your industry?

    d. What does the future of the industry look like?

    e. Are there trade associations connected with this industry that compile meaningful and available data?

5. Who is the customer?

    a. What are the relevant demographics?

    b. What is the customer's buying behavior?

    c. Why should the customer do business with the franchise?

6. How do you find customers?

    a. What are your advertising strategies?

    b. What are your marketing and public relations strategies?

    c. Do you attend trade shows? Which ones?

7. Where is the concept located?

    a. What type of location?

    b. What are the space requirements, build-out costs, etc.?

8. What is the profile of successful franchisee?

    a. What are the successful franchisee's traits, characteristics, experiences, strengths?

    b. What are the successful franchisee's background, education level, and aptitude?

    c. What are the successful franchisee's liquidity and net worth?

9. What are the investment options?

    a. What is the amount of money needed?

    b. What do franchisees receive in return?

    c. What can be financed?

    d. Where do franchisees obtain financing?

10. What support do franchisees get?

a. What support do franchisees get when finding a location?

b. What support do franchisees get when finding financing?

c. What support do franchisees get when undertaking construction?

d. What support do franchisees get concerning initial and ongoing training?

e. What support do franchisees get concerning marketing, graphic design, advertising, and promotional support?

f. What support do franchisees get concerning ongoing business coaching?

g. What support do franchisees get concerning product Research and Development?

One question that is not okay to ask, but is the big question to which everyone wants to know the answer is how much money you can make as a franchisee.

Franchisors cannot legally tell you *what you* will make because they do not know. Nobody has a crystal ball to predict his or her own future, let alone yours. If the franchisor tells you that it is illegal to tell you this, that is not completely accurate. In reality, a franchisor can tell you financial information as long as it is disclosed in Item 19 of their FDD and in accordance with FTC guidelines. About one third of all franchise companies disclose this information. Most quality franchisors have an earnings claim. A few of the reasons some do not have an earnings claim are logical:

1. They do not want you to know their numbers because the numbers are not good and would scare you away from buying their franchise

2. They do not have the ability to collect the data

3. They are worried they will get sued

Over time, it is highly probable that the companies that do not have an Item 19 earnings claim will add one in the interest of transparency and not to have a disadvantage against other franchise companies that do. Regardless, the best place to get more detailed information on what you can make is to speak with franchise owners. This is covered in greater detail later in the book. Approach your conversations with a franchisor in an open and honest way, and the understanding you will get of the franchisor's system will be significant. Adopting a cynical approach will very often not allow you to see the opportunities and possibilities in front of you. Keep an open mind until such time as you are shown why you should not keep it open. There is no reason to be cynical or reactionary to anything you come across in your franchise due diligence.

You can always tell someone to go to Hell tomorrow.

—Charlie Munger

A cynic is a coward. Cynicism always takes the easy way out. It is a form of laziness that provides someone with an excuse for not making any attempt to change. Cynicism is a way to hide. Cynics are afraid. So, instead, they pass judgment on anyone who is trying to make a difference. They ridicule the efforts of individuals and organizations that are working hard under incredibly difficult circumstances. Being cynical is often thought of as being composed and detached. It is considered to be a sign of sophistication. Cynics are mistakenly given credit for possessing a deep awareness regarding the limits of what humans can accomplish, which is somehow lacking in those who spend their time in passionate efforts to change the world. Being filled with cynicism is indeed a cowardly and sad way to go through life.

— Michael Crawley

ROCK 3 – UNDERSTANDING THE FRANCHISEE

A long conversation began, with Mark realizing how a franchise could potentially serve his dreams. Even though Mark initially thought that he should find a franchise that was in the finance sector because of his professional background, Sam told him he was being short sighted. Sam had the same orientation of going into a business that was closely related to his professional background but after understanding the characteristics that were most important to him, he went on a different path. After exploring the multitude of options, Sam found something that fit what he liked to do, and the market had a real need for the services that he could provide. Plus, he would get to deal with customers and run a business model others took time to develop. He could focus on the important parts of the business and have the franchisor focus on the back-office parts.

Sam had started the business doing most of the marketing and administrative work himself and was now at the point where he had a few employees. Sam seemed to really enjoy what he was doing, and he talked about the tax benefits of owning the business. It seemed like a foreign and exciting world to Mark, but Sam seemed to discuss it in very matter-of-fact terms.

"How did you find the franchise?" Mark asked. Sam had gotten the name of a franchise consultant from a cousin of his who had bought a franchise. The franchise consultant had significant experience in franchising. The consultant had worked with him to build a business model and then look at various companies that fit the criteria that were important to Sam. "He really helped me understand my options and made sure that I didn't look at companies that couldn't provide the kind of support that I found out I needed later on as I got the business started."

"I'm going to talk to my wife about this. I like the idea," Mark stated finally. The conversation ended shortly after.

Arriving home, he saw his wife and child waiting eagerly for him.

"What happened?" his wife said.

"Well, Sam seems happy with his decision to buy the franchise. He has a great team of people at the franchisors corporate office who are helping him grow and he feels he is in business for himself but not by himself. There are lots of different options out there, and he seems to be really successful. He gave me the name of a franchise consultant who helped him find the ideal franchise. I'm going to give him a call tomorrow."

"Mark. You know I support you in whatever you want to do. I just want to make sure we don't lose our house and can keep our finances secure. I'm really scared about the future. We had it good for so long, but the last few months have been really scary. It seems like we are living off money that we took years to save."

"Honey, I promise I'll make this work. I'm not going to find a job that is going to pay me what we need. I feel I'm at an age where employers think I'm too old and am going to cost them too much in insurance dollars. I'm at the point in my life where if I don't make opportunities happen for myself, no one is going to do it for me. Nobody is going to work harder for us than I am. I'm going to find out if this is viable and what it takes to make this happen. I'm going to call the guy Sam told me about and get some information about what it's like to own a franchise."

CHAPTER 11 - VALIDATING WITH FRANCHISEES

Calling franchise owners is one of the most important parts of your franchise due diligence, and a step that prospective candidates often rush through. My recommendation is to do the exact opposite! Rush to get to the step where the franchisor allows you to call franchise owners and then linger there for a bit. Call lots of franchise owners! This is a marvelous opportunity to get to learn what it is like to own and operate a business. What other investment allows you to go and look into your possible future by talking with people who have accomplished what you are looking to accomplish? There is, of course, a downside to this stage. It is now that you are under the highest scrutiny that you will encounter from the franchisor. In fact, many franchisors will terminate a due diligence when they clear a candidate to talk with their franchisees and then the candidate is lackadaisical, unorganized or disrespectful in their approach to doing so. Don't let your due diligence end before it really gets started because you thought you would put off for a few days your chance to call franchise owners as you did something that seemed more important at the time.

It is important to know that not only is the franchisor but also the current franchisees are going to be evaluating you just as thoroughly as you are evaluating them. Very often, if a candidate is rude, arrogant, or constantly focusing on negative aspects of the business, the franchisor is going to hear about it. This is a two-way investigation, and a quality franchisor is going to be attuned to what their franchisees have to say. Do not be the topic of an e-mail or a phone call from a franchise owner in the field telling the franchisor that you are not a good fit.

Here is a way you *do not* want the conversation to go: imagine this analogy—if you're a parent, you know that your child is the smartest and best looking in a classroom. In fact, isn't everyone's child the smartest and best looking (though not quite as smart or good looking as yours!) Now, imagine that you are bad mouthing someone's child and their parent overhears you. That parent is probably not going to have very warm feelings about you. Now think about the franchise in the same light. The franchise owners that you are speaking with have bought into the franchise vision. They have invested their time, energy, and financial resources into a business that they feel will take them to the level they want to reach. If you are undermining the franchisor, other franchisees, or the business, you are actually undermining that particular franchisee as well, saying not only that the franchisee's kid is ugly and stupid but the franchisee is as well! Not a great way to get the information that we are looking for.

You will find most franchise owners are very willing to take time from their business day to talk with you. Often I have had individuals comment on how incredibly helpful these franchise owners were to them in their search. The amount of information a franchise owner is willing to share when he or she believes that you are truly interested in owning the franchise is astounding. From walking through every aspect of their experiences to their finances to their vision, what franchise owners are willing to share may be much more than you may expect. The reason most franchise owners will do this is that they were once in your seat. They were trying to figure out the answers to the same questions you have now. They want to tell you their story, warts and all. Those questions may include the following:

1. Will I love doing this?
2. Can I do this successfully?

3. Will I make the kind of money I need to make?
4. What kinds of people are associated with this franchise system?

The truth is that if you approach these business owners from a place of honesty and respect, they will help you. It is human nature to reciprocate and they will honor your respect by inviting you into their businesses, they will send you information that you may not believe someone would make available to a stranger, they will give you tips that they picked up, and they will give you a glimpse into what your life may be like as a franchisee. I have asked many franchise owners why they do this, and their answers are candid:

1. Someone helped me in my search.
2. I want to make sure that the people who are coming into *my* brand share the same vision that my franchisor partner and I do.
3. I want to *grow my* brand, and the best way to do it is with strong franchisee partners across the entire system.

Wow! What a great group of people we can talk with. A good way to think of the vibe you should be feeling after talking with franchise owners is simple. Have you ever been to a party, and you met some friends of a friend? You end up speaking with them for hours in the kitchen, and on the way out you think to yourself, "What great people—I would like to see them again!" Keep that thought in mind. If you are talking with people of a like mind, you will enjoy being a part of that system. You will find value in your continued conversations with them after you join the franchise. You will meet them at the conventions, at the regional meetings in your focused peer groups, and you will enjoy interacting with them. They will become your friends and confidants. You will be a part of the same organization, and the values you have, the goals you are striving towards, will be similar to what they are striving for. In short, you will be part of a team.

How to Start

Remember, we are on the third stone, so we have successfully understood from the franchisor what their business is all about. We understand how they make money, what their operations look like, and what their vision is. It is critical that before we talk with franchise owners, we have a strong understanding of their system. If you do not know how the franchise works and what activities are important to making money, you will get very little value from your conversations with franchise owners. More importantly, you will be wasting their time and yours. The franchise owners do not have to talk with you. They are not being compensated to talk with you. You are actually costing them money because for every minute they talk with you, they are taking a minute out of their business.

I've had clients who called me during this phase and said "that franchise owner was rude – he hung up on me!" When I asked why, it usually becomes very obvious that the level of preparation wasn't sufficient for the franchise owner to continue the conversation. The franchise owner's role here is not to teach you everything about the business, it is to answer your specific and intelligent questions. They are not trying to sell you the franchise, they are trying to help you understand their reality. And they are actually paying you for the privilege to help you! Here is a way to think of it. If a franchise owner is making a $100,000 a year and working two thousand hours, every hour of their time is worth $50. If they are making $1,000,000 a year, every hour is worth $500. If a complete stranger is willing to invest that kind of money into you, you should not waste that person's time.

> *If you love life, don't waste time, for time is what life is made up of.*
> - Bruce Lee
> -

As part of your due diligence, the franchisor will make their network available to you. You can find a listing of names and phone numbers of all of the franchisees in the FDD, on their Web site, or the franchisor can send you a list. If franchisors will not help you with this step, you should seriously consider dropping your franchise investigation. You are looking for a full and transparent partnership. Anyone withholding information, whether it is you, the franchisor, or the existing franchisees, is not a good sign.

Very often, the franchisor will give you a password or phrase that you can tell the franchisee so they know that you are a real candidate actively looking at this system and not a competitor or someone who has not spent the time to learn about what they do. This should not be viewed as the franchisor trying to control your conversations—it is really a defense mechanism to protect the franchisees' time. I view this as admirable. When you are in business, you would not want a steady stream of people asking you about your business if they were not seriously interested in becoming a part of it, or if they were a competitor trying to understand what your business model was.

Who to talk with

$$\alpha = \log_4 5 \approx 1.16$$

The Pareto Principle (also known as the 80–20 rule, the law of the vital few, and the principle of factor sparsity) states that, for many events, roughly 80 percent of the effects come from 20 percent of the causes.

Vilfredo Pareto observed in 1906 that 80 percent of the land in Italy was owned by 20 percent of the people; he further established the principle by observing that 20 percent of the pea pods in his garden had 80 percent of the peas.

Why are peas and an equation important when thinking about who to talk within a franchise? Simple: we are looking to talk with the people who are actively achieving results utilizing the franchise system you are interested in becoming a part of. In any franchise system, 20 percent of the franchisees are going to be doing great, 60 percent are going to be earning a solid livelihood, and 20 percent are going to be on the path to closing or selling the franchise because it did not work out for them. You probably know the 80-20 rule and how it holds true to many aspects of life. Here are a few you will find in talking with franchise owners:

- 80 percent of your profits come from 20 percent of your customers
- 80 percent of your complaints come from 20 percent of your customers
- 80 percent of your profits come from 20 percent of the time you spend improving the business
- 80 percent of your sales come from 20 percent of your products
- 80 percent of your sales are made by 20 percent of your sales staff

Let us spend our time wisely. We are going to want to talk with a few franchisees who are doing great, a few who are doing okay, and a few who are not doing so well. The important aspect that we must remember is that you need to understand the system well enough that when you see success, you understand what part of the franchise system and model it is coming from, and when you see failure, you see where the franchisee might be deviating from what the franchisor's recipe is.

The Flying Leap of Greed or Fear

A common trap for franchise candidates is to talk with people who are successful and not understand *why* and *how* they are using the franchise model to gain their success. If you only look at results and think merely by buying the franchise, you will attain the same results, you are setting yourself up for failure. If the people you are talking with are successful because they share certain traits that you do not have, enjoy doing something that you hate to do, or are following a process that you cannot follow, why do you think you would be successful owning that kind of business? Just because someone is doing something and succeeding at it does not mean that you will succeed as well. If you hate doing something, nothing is going to change after you buy the business. You will find reasons *not* to do the things that make the other franchisees successful, and you will start down the road to failure, despite your fellow franchisees' success. This is often the fate of those poor souls who purchase a franchise based upon some esoteric list and not after conducting a thorough due diligence.

Another common variation on this scenario is someone talking with franchise owners who are unsuccessful and not understanding where they are not following the system. The person who does this will think that the franchisor or the system is not successful and shut themselves down. Do not let yourself fall into either trap. You are looking to gain experience and insight from people. If you do not understand why something is working or not working, ask the franchisor. Get the franchisor's side of the story. Balance what you are hearing, and you will be very close to the truth. Do not assume that the franchisor is telling you one thing and the "reality" is what is going on out in the field with the franchise owners. This is an attitude I have witnessed many times, and it is very self-destructive. If you do not trust the franchisor and trust the franchisees more—this is a big mistake. You are looking for reasons for failure and not looking for success. You are looking for reasons not to buy the franchise and not for how the franchise can get you closer to your goals. This is a mindset born of fear. Usually the fear is that you will fail at the franchise business, so you start looking for reasons to move away from the issue that you view as harmful. You justify your fear by thinking and saying, "The franchise model is no good. Nobody is making money. If I do this, I will not make money either!" If you find yourself coming to this conclusion multiple times you may have one of two things going on; either you are looking at terrible companies or you are not really cut out for owning a business.

Life Cycle and Location of Business

In any franchise, you are going to have franchisees in varying stages of their business existence. Think of analyzing this like you would a mutual fund. Take a look at one-year, three-year and five-year performance. The newer franchisees are going to be very close to their initial training and start-up experiences and will be able to tell you a lot about what the start-up process is like. The older the franchise, the more the franchisees can tell you about what it is like to run a more stabilized business. We want to get a balanced viewpoint across the years and not focus too much on any particular part of the growth curve. We want to understand the positives and negatives associated with the various stages of the lifecycle of the franchise. If you only talk with long-term existing franchise owners, you are letting "survivorship bias" creep into your mind, and you will not really understand the ups and downs of what it takes to become a successful franchisee.

"If in state, won't validate". If you want to get a knowing laugh from the corporate team at just about any franchise company, repeat this adage to them. You will find it to be very true. Usually, the first person a franchise candidate wants to talk with or mystery shop is the franchise in their city or in their state. Resist the urge to do this. Very often, you will find that the local franchisee is not really thrilled about you coming into their backyard. Maybe the franchisee is doing substantial business where you are looking to open your business, and if you come in, the franchisee will lose that revenue to you. To protect their interests and block your intentions, the existing franchisee may call the franchisor and ask them to have the rights to buy the new franchise unit- leaving the newcomer with nothing to buy. This happens much more often than is realized and usually results in the existing franchise owner buying the territory out from under you despite the fact that the franchisor would prefer you have it.

Why would the franchisor want a new franchise owner in an area instead of automatically asking the existing franchisee if they want to run another location within the same area? Simply put, franchise theory shows that having multiple operators within a geographic area diminishes the risk for the entire enterprise. The theory puts forth that having multiple operators produces more marketing money to develop the brand, and there is more opportunity for group purchasing power. Very often, a new franchise owner will think, "If only I owned the entire market, I could grow to be a huge business." Sometimes that is true, but most of the time, if that franchise owner does not have the resources to fully develop the market, the additional territory the franchise owner has lays fallow and does not generate any benefit to them or the franchisor. The power of many aligned participants in a brand is good for the whole.

This sounds logical. However, sometimes, between theoretical logic and the real world, greed creeps in. I have seen it many times, and you probably have as well. Be careful of talking with the local franchise. You can get just as much information by talking with a franchise in a neighboring state or a similar market without having to worry that the territory you are looking at will become unavailable. Of course, it may be important to meet the neighbor. If that is the case, be sure you have a commitment from the franchisor that they will not sell the territory out from under you. Get this in writing to avoid any confusion. This does not obligate you to purchase the franchise but it does bring a level of clarity to the exercise.

After you join the franchise, the franchisor will certainly facilitate the meeting of the local brands, and most franchisors have a protocol for doing this in order to create cohesive partnerships between the local franchise owners. Ask the franchisor what this protocol is and how the franchisor will help bring you into their local system. If we're not careful, we may find ourselves in a position to let a neighboring franchise owner negatively influence our perception of the business or act in such a way that is more to their benefit than yours. Remember, "If in state, won't validate!"

Franchisees who are Closing and Selling

In any mature franchise, there are going to be businesses that are selling or closing. You can learn a lot by speaking with these franchisees, and if they are in your local market, you may be able to purchase a going concern. Of course, it is important to know *why* they are selling. There are several possible reasons a business could be for sale—both positive and negative. Our job is to understand which is which.

1. Is the franchisee retiring and selling at a profit?
2. Is the franchisee failing and desperately trying to get out?
3. Is the franchise system a failure?
4. Has something in the regulatory or local environment changed that is hurting business?
5. Is it a health issue?

If it is a local business and you are thinking of buying it, this is a good time to visit with that individual. Spend time in this person's business; get to know what it is all about. You will find that the more face time you have with the owner, the higher quality your analysis will be. If the business is for sale at a premium and it is worth it, you are buying cash flow. If the business is for sale at a discount and it is a logical reason, you are getting an asset for a good price. If the business is for sale because the franchisor is a failure and does not support the business because it had no chance of ever really succeeding you are buying a time bomb. Shut the book on that investigation and *run away!*

Tactics: What to Ask Them and How

Any franchise owner that is going to bring you value through a conversation is going to be a busy franchise owner. Make the franchise owner's life easy. I recommend you e-mail franchise owners asking for a time that is convenient for them to talk. Do not send your questions to them and expect them to diligently fill out the answers. What you will end up with is a bunch of no-replies to your email and a bunch of franchise owners who think you are too lazy to spend any time getting to know them.

Ask the same questions across a range of franchise owners so that you can gain an understanding of the consistency across the network. If you ask the question "Would you do this again?" and you get a constant stream of "NO," that is probably a good thing to know. On the other hand, you will likely not have the time to ask all the questions you want answered. Budget your time accordingly and realize that the franchise owner is busy trying to run a business. Be respectful of the franchise owner's time. You will find that there are some franchise owners you make great connections with. You can always ask if you can call them again. Sending a note or a small gift is a nice way to have the privilege of having another conversation with someone. I have found that sending a bottle of red wine or flowers tends to be the fastest way to show your appreciation of a kind gesture and it usually guarantees that second phone call or in person visit with someone who is busy building their own business.

Leave a trail of friends while you are talking with franchise owners. It is nice to meet these people at the annual convention and have them remember you as a class act. It is great to start off your franchise career with people who can help you and perhaps become lifelong friends.

Over the years, I have met many prospective franchise owners who have asked great questions, and I have these available for you to start compiling your own research. The great thing about this stage of the due diligence is that the more questions you ask, the more empowered you will become and your understanding of the business increases exponentially.

For a list of questions you may find helpful in your conversations with franchise owners, feel free to visit:

www.TheFranchiseMBA.com.

CHAPTER 12 - FRANCHISE DEVELOPMENT

What walks on four legs in the morning, two legs in the afternoon, and three legs at night?

This is the riddle of the Sphinx. The Sphinx at Thebes would pose this question to travelers; if they failed to solve it, they were killed. I am here to help you answer it correctly to conquer the Sphinx, or in your case, the franchise riddle. The answer is a human.

How is this Applicable to Franchise Development?

At the beginning of life, a baby crawls on all fours. Similarly, you as the franchisee are largely dependent on your team and franchisor for support. During the middle of life, the human walks on two legs. In the franchise context, at this stage you have broken down the franchise system to make it fit you, your preferences, and your expectations perfectly. Still, you are new to the business of franchising, and you have a lot of questions about franchising itself and whether it is right for you. The human, at the end of his life, walks on three legs (with a cane). The cane symbolizes the knowledge that is accumulated over a lifetime.

Any sort of start-up business, whether it is a franchise or something else, is going to be an emotional roller coaster. While on this rollercoaster, one day you will be convinced that you are the king of the world, and the next you are an abject failure who is about to ruin his life for good. This is called the "transition curve," and if you embrace this and understand what your emotional responses are going to be, you will be empowered to understand where you are in your personal development.

The next part of your growth is going to be where you are in relation to your franchisor-franchisee partnership. As you go through the six stages of franchise development, as defined by Greg Sam, the founder of the Franchise Relationships Institute, you will be empowered with the knowledge and comfort that you have made the right decision and your franchise is running how it should. Chart your goals carefully, and as you encounter the ups and downs along the way, you can keep your eyes on what is really important to you.

If you want to live a happy life, tie it to a goal, not to people or things.

—Albert Einstein

The Transition Curve

Think of the emotional roller coaster you're about to go through. Keep this image in mind. Have you ever been on an airplane that hits an air pocket? One moment you are sitting comfortably in your seat, the next moment you feel as if the plane is about to drop out of the sky. You will most certainly hit air pockets in your quest for a business. Your emotions are going to peak and plummet, and then you will be faced with an option of either quitting or making this endeavor work. Understand the emotions that are about to come into play, and you will be better equipped to deal with them and not be sidetracked by your animal instincts.

Transition Curve

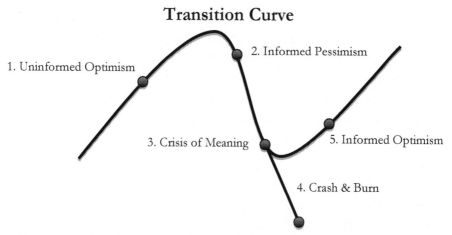

Stage 1: The first stage of the concept is called "Uninformed Optimism."

At this stage, you have just come on board. You own the business. You're a new franchisee. You wear your crisp logoed shirts with pride. Everyone you meet gets a business card. You are excited. You have taken the first steps to your independence. You are on top of the world. This is a great feeling.

Stage 2: The second stage is called "Informed Pessimism."

Imagine a roller coaster about to crest the top and go down. You are starting to feel a little worried about this decision you made to enter into a franchise relationship. Everything seemed so exciting before, but now the bills are starting to pile up. Feelings of fear, nervousness, and frustration begin to set in. Sometimes you have days where you win a big sale or land a good account. Sometimes you feel like the world is out to get you. You are alternately scared and excited.

Stage 3: The third stage is called "Crisis of Meaning."

This is a scary place. You're not sleeping well at night. You feel like this endeavor could backfire. Your family's future is at stake, and you're not sure if you can make ends meet. Even though you know there are other franchise owners out there who are doing well, you talk with franchise owners who are in the same boat as you, and you feel like maybe you're not really cut out for this. Customers aren't buying as fast as you had projected. The business is starting to not look certain. Perhaps you even start thinking of what it would be like to sell the business. Maybe you should have taken that job instead of buying a franchise. You are accelerating downward, and you're not sure if you can keep on the tracks.

Crash and burn at this point, and the business will probably not survive. You can hit the bottom of this curve and go off the rails. In that case, your business will fail and you will lose your investment. There is a whole litany of negative things that can happen if this is the case. On the flip side, you can take your forward momentum and harness it. Just like a roller coaster car can achieve a velocity that will propel it into the next upswing, so can you propel yourself out of your descent and start climbing back up. This is the Crisis of Meaning. Every successful business owner has gone through the Crisis of Meaning. Just ask them. They will tell you all about it. The common thread for how they survived their Crisis of Meaning is usually that they made the decision that they weren't going to fail. As simple as that sounds, making the decision to survive and succeed is one of the most powerful forces that a human being can muster. We all have it within us. After all, we are all survivors. Thousands of our ancestors figured out how to survive in order for you to get to this point. We all have survivor genes within us. You can make it if you will it to be so. The Crisis of Meaning will make you stronger, but that doesn't mean that it is any less scary or painful.

Stage 4: Informed Optimism.

You are back on track. Your business is starting to come along in the right direction. You are making money. You see the opportunity. You do not feel like you are about to lose the business. You see the pot of gold at the end of the rainbow. There is hope after all!

As you go through your own emotional rollercoaster, you will also be concurrently progressing through six stages of a relationship with the franchisor.

Six Stages of Franchise Development:

If you have committed to your new business and are prepared to continue with it through the cyclical ups and downs, it is inevitable that you will go through these six stages of franchise development. Greg Nathan is credited with developing this framework for the "6-Stages of Franchise Relationships". He's an internationally recognized psychological expert on the franchisor / franchisee relationship. How you go through these stages is up to you. A positive attitude will benefit you. That is why I am sharing this knowledge with you so you pass through these stages as painlessly as possible.

The Glee Stage

The glee stage takes place when you sign the papers and get the keys to your new business. The business is now yours. You are very happy with the relationship that you have with your franchisor. You are excited about your new business. Along with your decision to enter into a relationship with a franchisor, you wonder how things will work out and hope to make tons of money. This is the stage where the franchisor will provide you with encouragement and support, their new franchisee, till death do us part. In this stage, positive emotions run high, and there is a clear vision and expectation of achievement as the hurdles of starting the business are put behind you. This stage starts when you are in the process of signing the papers with your franchisor and lasts approximately six months.

The Fee Stage

Now that you have started making money with your business, you look at where that money goes and examine the operation more closely. You observe that although you are making money, these royalty payments and franchising fees really cut into your profit. While there might be high average unit volume (AUV) in stores, when you boil down your earnings after expenses, it may be very different from your expectations. Managing expectations is very important. This stage continues with you throughout the business as you get a better handle on the business's finances. You may start asking yourself what you are really getting for your money, and your level of satisfaction with your franchisor may drop. This stage may lead back into the Glee Stage if your franchisor provides assistance with a cutback on fees, additional support or some other benefit but it usually leads into the "Me Stage."

The Me Stage

The Me Stage is where you, the franchisee, question your dependence on the franchisor. Along with evaluating your financial statements to understand your income and expenses better, you wonder if you could be as successful or maybe even more successful without your franchisor. As you put in the hard work and effort, succeeding as a result, you fall into the self-serving bias. The self-serving bias says that as you perform well or achieve something, you attribute it to your own skills and personality, which is reasonable. It is you who owns the business, and you deserve credit. There is another side to this. If your business is not performing up to your expectations, you will tend to blame someone else. This exists strongly in the franchisor-franchisee relationship. When things are going well, you attribute them to your own hard work. When things are not going as planned, you attribute them to the shortfalls of your franchisor and the franchisor's lack of support. The criticism that you develop can put a strain on your relationship if it is not carefully articulated to the franchisor. This leads to the Free Stage.

The Free Stage

Just how a baby requires love and support until the baby is older and prepared to handle the world on his or her own, the same applies to the franchisee. As you develop and mature as a franchisee, you may be frustrated by the support and regulation from your franchisor. You start viewing the franchisor's rules less as support guidelines and more like restrictions; after all, you want to be able to personalize your business and express your own ideas. Your business confidence has grown as you have achieved success. This builds the need to assert yourself as you go seeking independence.

The Free Stage is characterized by trying to test your restrictions and limitations by pushing the system's boundaries. You want to see if you can break free of some of your contractual obligations. This is the most dangerous stage of franchise ownership. The franchisor is an equal party in your contract and might decide to break free of your franchise either through a forced sale or termination of the agreement. You can either get stuck in this stage, which like the relationship between a rebellious teenager and his parents leads to trouble for both, or you get to the See Stage.

The See Stage

The See Stage is the transition between walking on two feet and walking on three. You have been given the cane of knowledge. In the See Stage, you see the value of the franchisor's support services and the importance of following the system. You understand why you have to follow the system and see the competitive edge of being part of a healthy franchise system.

In order for you to get through the See Stage, you need to be open with your franchisor and share why you feel like you are being restricted. It is important that both you and the franchisor listen carefully to what each other has to say and share your insights. This might open old wounds, but the understanding that you gain from accepting and letting go of the past can help heal your relationship. It can improve your relationship if the franchisor is more open to using the franchisee's advice going forward in growing the brand. The knowledge gained from going through these five stages lead to the We Stage.

The We Stage

As you develop your relationship further with your franchisor, you come to appreciate and see the potential that you have together—you grow together. You might need some specific help to grow your business, and you can also share your ideas for the franchisor to strengthen the brand.

The main difference between the See Stage and We Stage is the thought process; you move from independent to interdependent thinking. This requires maturity, objectivity, and with respect to your business, profitability. Only if you are making money will you be satisfied with your franchisor. The franchisor also must fulfill its obligations, be adaptable, and be fair and consistent in its dealings.

Once you are in the sixth stage, you will be happy to work with your franchisor, and your franchisor will consider you a great asset. As you build a healthy business relationship with your franchisor, you will also develop relationships with your peers, employees, and customers. As always, deliver the experience in the store that keeps people coming back. If you do not deliver the experience, the customers will walk right by your store and your progress will revert.

Starting a business is not easy. Neither is raising kids. Most things in life that are worth having are not easy, but when you accomplish them you are a better person for it. Your pride in building a business, creating a family, or raising children is something that you will be proud of every day of your life.

All the adversity I've had in my life, all my troubles and obstacles, have strengthened me... You may not realize it when it happens, but a kick in the teeth may be the best thing in the world for you.

—Walt Disney

CHAPTER 13 - UNDERSTANDING FRANCHISE SUCCESS

The greatest franchises of our time have left their mark on societies, and they continue to flourish all over the world. Brands like McDonald's, Subway, Meineke, 7-Eleven, and Supercuts dominate their respective industries, but what have these franchises done to have such a strong track record?

This chapter presents eight key traits that made these entities successful.

1. Targeted Customer Feedback

Feedback is necessary for improvement, but most of the feedback good franchises receive may be viewed as trivial. We can look at feedback from the perspective of the diffusion of innovations, a concept that was developed to describe how people buy into new products.

The Diffusion of Innovation

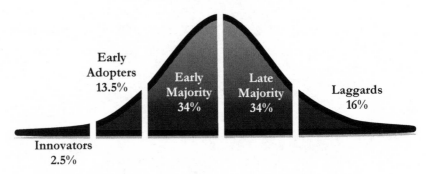

Source: EM Rogers, Diffusion of Innovations 4th Edition. New York the Free Press (1995)

Feedback will come from people who come from many of these perspectives. The innovators and early adopters will provide feedback that is long term in nature because they are the ones who try the product before the main-stream audiences grab it. They see visions of what an entity could become, and their input tends to be the most valuable in the earlier stages of a franchise. As a franchise develops, the early and late majority provide feedback that stabilize the entity's growth and distinguish its brand. Depending on the kind of franchise you are pursuing, and depending on what stage it is in, make sure you understand the feedback that the franchisor is accumulating. A good ear is needed to decipher what truly matters for the franchise's success. You do not want to listen to innovators once they have captured a large market share—you want to ensure the large market share stays satisfied. Change from a business system standpoint should be gradual.

2. Adapting, Not Changing

The whole point of the franchise model is that the system works almost everywhere. If the franchisor is doing a complete 180-degree turn from time to time, it is safe to assume that the franchisor does not have the track record to be a successful franchise. There will always be valuable input and data from customers and employees in a business that can improve the efficiency and output of that business, but it is important to remember that this input is not meant to revolutionize the entity. There needs to be some continuity for a franchise system to create a brand. Small adaptations to your climate can be beneficial, but completely changing the entity or operating model is usually a bad sign.

3. Brand Recognition

Brands need visionary promises, extraordinary delivery, and very measurable results. They need to reflect the core of the franchise, beyond all of its frills and perks.

—Edward Leaman, CEO of Growers and Nomads

This is by far one of the most important, if not the most important, assets a franchise has. Without a brand to recognize, the growth of a franchise is slowed. There needs to be some unique flavor to a franchise that keeps customers wanting more. Whatever that may be, from the decor of the entity to the style of the service, these unique attributes are a small piece of the brand. Coupled with its grander mission and visions, franchises continue to prosper. Logos and advertising play a key role in showcasing the brand, and the more a franchise markets itself to the public, the better it is for its franchisee. Having a powerful brand does not mean that those without powerful brands cannot succeed; however, those with accurate and powerful branding succeed more often.

4. More Support Services

Franchises with national conventions and mentor programs are successful because franchises want to learn from each other about the mistakes, errors, or successes they have had.

—Todd Leff, CEO of Hand and Stone Massage

All great franchises have spent considerable time and resources to achieve a developed model. They may have started with less support services initially, but as they grow, their support structures expand, and their operations manuals spell everything out. The best franchisors know exactly what matters for a franchisees' success, and they will share thorough information. Franchisees require experience and advice throughout this process.

5. Long-Term Contracts

Franchisors that trust their product or services vitality will create longer-term contracts with franchisees than those who do not. This stems from a sheer trust in their system. Plus, having a longer-term contract allows more equity to vest in a franchise, and it allows the franchisee to see the value they will have in the future. No matter what terms and obligations a franchisor offers, pay close attention to how long a contract is. The typical contracts are for ten years with the right to extend in five-year increments. Remember, if you do not extend a franchise contract, you lose all equity that is vested in the franchise. The best options when you do not want to run a franchise is to place a manager in the system and create an annuity for yourself, or sell the business and exit completely.

6. Registered with State Authorities

All state authorities have a registration process for franchise entities. These processes vary from state to state, and the requisite paperwork is different. Contact the Federal Trade Commission or your state authority to ensure a franchise has the right to develop in a region. Those that are registered in more states tend to be more successful over time. They have a vision of expanding well beyond just their home state, and they usually register in multiple states very quickly. Over time, they may look to develop their brand internationally as well as domestically.

7. Internationally Minded

The percentage of successful franchise systems looking to expand overseas has increased substantially over the years. An entity's international presence is more than just a sign of success—it is also an indicator of increased stability. No country in existence today has permanent growth or decline, and establishing entities on an international stage helps the franchise's bottom line by diversifying the revenue stream across different countries. In addition, the diversification of ideas that flow across different countries borders is a significant resource to all the franchise owners in a system.

8. Sufficient Amounts of Capital

More money means more opportunity, expansion, and security; however, the company's assets need to be evaluated in relation to the company's debts. A franchise should have enough money to cover unexpected expenses. Analyze the company's reserves to ensure that they are financially stable. Some companies have lower costs, and some have higher costs. Knowing which ones have which capital strengths is important. You never want to invest in a company that has a financial position that you are not comfortable with, and more mature franchisors typically have large amounts of cushion in their assets.

These eight attributes have been proven effective across the board for franchisors.

Though a track record is helpful, it is important to realize that the individual contributes quite a bit to business success. These traits mean nothing without a visionary person at the helm, ready to hold on and face the imminent challenges. Running a business takes personal understanding and commitments.

Summary

The best franchises of our world have a system in place, and consistent expansion is their goal. They are registered with all the required governmental entities, and they keep money on hand to cover mistakes. In addition, they hire specialists to help their franchisees prosper. At the end of the day, however, it is the individual people who own the franchises that make all the difference.

ROCK 4 – LEGAL AND FINANCIAL DETAILS

CHAPTER 14 - THE FDD

Details create the big picture.

—Sandy Weill, CEO of Citibank

Some people say they see poetry in my paintings. I see only science.

—Georges Seurat

Before you can purchase a franchise, you will receive an approximately two hundred-page document known as the Franchise Disclosure Document, or FDD. It is composed of twenty-three sections called "items." The Federal Trade Commission mandates that a franchisor must furnish this to their candidates at least fourteen days prior to the sale of a franchise. It is full of information about the history of the franchise, mutual obligations, and other data pertaining to the company you are interested in buying.

There are also a number of states that require franchisors to register their opportunity and that give franchise buyers certain legal rights. These states have franchise investment laws that require additional disclosure requirements. In essence, these states treat the sale of a franchise like the sale of a security.

The FDD is a marvelous document and is one of the key reasons why franchising has been so successful. You can achieve a level of transparency through the FDD that is not possible in other investments or in business opportunities. Contained within the FDD is information on legal issues that may have occurred, backgrounds of the corporate executives, financial representations, current franchise owners' names and phone numbers, and the names of franchise owners who have left the system. There is a lot of juicy information here!

You cannot just call a franchisor and ask for the franchise's FDD. You usually need to be a candidate that the franchisor has expressed an interest in by approving your application.

Compare the FDD to a pointillist painting, composed of thousands of small dots. Looking at it from afar, it is a harmonious and comprehensive subject. The point of this chapter is to help you look at the dots in the painting closely to understand how they all work together.

Oftentimes, if the Franchisor perceives you to be serious, they will send you an FDD immediately. My recommendation is to not read the FDD until you understand the business by research you have done and after talking with other franchisees.

I know that sounds counterintuitive, but you will probably run away from the business if you read the FDD before you understand the business model and how it has run by others. It is scary. It is pretty one-sided (it was written by the franchisor's lawyers after all). Reading the FDD will not teach you the business any more than it will help you understand the moral character of the franchisor or the business activities of your fellow franchisees. After all, what is the point of reading and understanding the FDD only to find that you don't like the franchisor nor the franchisees in the system?

When we talked about looking at owning a franchise as crossing a stream, we stated that there are four rocks that we will step on to get across:

Rock 1: Introspective Self – Know Yourself

Rock 2: Knowledge of the Franchisor

Rock 3: Knowledge of the Franchisee

Rock 4: Legal/Financial Issues

This is the last rock. Of course, this rock is as important as any of the other rocks because it still holds the promise of getting us to the other side, but it could just as easily cause us fall into the water! In fact, sometimes the promise of being so close to the other side causes people to go through this step rapidly. That is a mistake as well. We will definitely want to spend time learning and understanding every document that we agree to before purchasing a franchise because from the beginning, we have to understand the big picture.

So put away that FDD until you know that you like the business, like the people, and can actually see yourself owning and running this franchise.

Now that we have set the framework for how to view the FDD, let us take a closer look at what the FDD includes.

A franchise disclosure document (FDD) is a legal document that is presented to prospective buyers of franchises in the presale disclosure process in the United States. It was originally known as the Uniform Franchise Offering Circular (UFOC) or uniform franchise disclosure document, prior to revisions made by the Federal Trade Commission in July 2007. While I cannot confirm my suspicions, I think they changed the name to FDD from UFOC because if you say the letters UFOC as a word, it is distasteful and crass.

You should know the FDD inside and out before making a decision concerning whether to enter into a business relationship with any franchise. Hiring a franchise attorney to review the document is a good idea if you do not understand what you are reading or if the franchisor cannot give you a reasonable explanation as to why something is in there. In fact, if the franchisor cannot give you a reasonable explanation, you may want to seriously reconsider why you are looking at this franchise.

When you receive the FDD, you will see that the information is divided into a cover page, table of contents, and the twenty-three items.

There are twenty-three different sections within a standard FDD:

Item 1: The Franchisor, Predecessors and Affiliates

This section describes the type of business and its history, such as mergers and acquisitions, and discloses corporate information, such as the headquarters location.

Questions to ask yourself:

- Was this business spun out of another business, and why?
- How old is this business?
- Does the history of the company seem congruent with what the company is describing?

Item 2: The Franchisor, Predecessors and Affiliates

This section identifies all key personnel and affiliates who play a significant role in business operations and their business experience over the past five years

Questions to ask yourself:

- Are you comfortable with key personnel's business experience?
- If they have had a series of non-related jobs, why?

- When you ask them about their background, do they have a series of increasingly responsible positions?

Item 3: Litigation

This section details the history of criminal, civil, and administrative litigation involving the business or any of the officers, owners, directors, or executives of the company.

Some litigation is to be expected. We live in a litigious society. Red flags show up when there is a concentration of litigation in a short period of time. You can always call the people who are involved in a lawsuit. Unless they signed a mutual release that involves a confidentiality clause, you may be able to learn a lot about the business. Take it with a grain of salt though; there are always two sides to a story. Listen to both sides before you come to a conclusion.

Questions to ask yourself:

- Are there a large number of lawsuits involving this company?
- Are the lawsuits due to the market, the operator, or the franchisor?
- What is the character of the officers? Shoddy ethics and low integrity are good reasons to walk away from an opportunity.

Item 4: Bankruptcy

This section reveals if any of the company directors or officers have filed for bankruptcy during the past fifteen years, and if so, what were the circumstances and outcomes. If there are bankruptcies here, you should be very careful.

Questions to ask yourself:

- Why would you want to partner with someone who has shown a willingness to walk away from his or her obligations? If there is a bankruptcy on file, walk away.

Item 5: Initial Franchise Fees

This section states what the initial fees are to buy the franchise, how the money is used, and what, if any, refund is available should the agreement not be fulfilled.

Questions to ask yourself:

- Are the fees in the agreement the same as those described by the franchisor in your previous conversations? If the fees are different or you were offered some inducements, like a free trip or extra support in some area, be sure to get that in writing in an addendum that goes into your contract.

Item 6: Other Fees

This section discloses all fees and payments required of the franchisee, such as royalties, insurance, advertising, training, and any other payments due to the franchisor.

Questions to ask yourself:

- Where is the money going?
- Are there services that the franchisor is offering that you have to use that you could source locally for a lower cost?

○ Some examples would be phone-answering and other support services. Be sure that these are warranted and effective. The easiest way is to ask the franchisor and then ask the franchisees what their opinion is of these services, i.e. are they quality services that pay for themselves, or are they a revenue stream for the franchisor that are forced onto the franchisees

Item 7: Estimated Initial Investment

This section estimates how much the franchisee can expect to invest in equipment, supplies, real estate, furnishings, working capital, and other costs associated with starting up the business..

Questions to ask yourself:

- Do I understand my costs? This will be expressed as a range reported to the franchisor. Be sure to understand where you fall in these numbers by creating a pro forma budget of expenses. An easy way to do this is to ask franchise owners if they would be willing to share information about their start-up costs with you in an Excel document, then consider that information in conjunction with the costs in your local market. As an example, real estate is going to cost more in New York City than it is in Cleveland. Let us make sure you know where you fall on the spectrum of costs.
- What were franchise owners' start-up costs? When talking with other franchise owners, ask them for their start-up expenses, compare this to the Item 7,

and look for discrepancies. Are there expenses that you should account for more fully? Ask yourself how you spend money and whether you will have a light or heavy touch when it comes to spending money on the business. As an example, I have seen franchise owners who purchase new office equipment because it is important they project a certain look. I have seen other franchise owners who purchase their equipment used. There are always lots of places to save money if that is the kind of person that you are.

Item 8: Restrictions and Obligations on Products and Services

This section describes the designated sources the franchisee must use for equipment, supplies, and services, and whether the franchisor earns revenue from these designated sources.

Questions to ask yourself:

- Is the franchisor treating their designated sources ethically and in a fashion that you find beneficial to you? This is always an interesting section. One of the prime benefits of franchising is that you are able to be part of a group of businesses, which should lower your expenses on items that are necessary for the business. Sometimes, franchisors abuse this to create additional revenue opportunities for themselves, so be aware of this possibility.
  - o Is what the franchisor selling you equal to or better than what is available on the free market?

- o Is the price equal to or better than what is available?

- o Are you a captive buyer for the franchisor, i.e., is the franchisor really a manufacturer that is going to force you to buy a certain quantity of something it manufactures? Is that a position you are comfortable with?

- o If the franchise company manufacturers something that is necessary in the fulfillment of your product or service, ask yourself if this is a world- class product. Is it available elsewhere for the same cost? If the franchisor purchases this from a third party and renames it, is there protection from that third party selling it elsewhere?

- Oftentimes, especially with franchisors that are selling you something that you have to use in the delivery of your product or service, there are significant restrictions on what you can and cannot sell. Make sure you understand these restrictions and that these restrictions are logical and beneficial to everyone in the network. A good way to test this is to ask yourself, "If a neighboring franchise were not following this, would it hurt my business?"

- How much revenue does the franchisor earn from selling things to their franchisees? Is this greater than what the franchisor earns on royalties? Are you more comfortable with a franchisor that earns money when your business is growing revenue or one that views you as a customer, and the bigger you become the more you buy,? Neither is right or wrong—it all depends on your view and how this relationship plays out in practice with the franchisor. If the franchisor forces the franchisees to purchase materials when you don't need them and the benefit is a one way street to the franchisor, that is probably not a good position to be in. A few conversations with franchisees will generally reveal what the reality is. Franchisor or franchise-czar?

Item 9: Franchisee's Obligations

This section details the specifications for anything the franchisee must lease or purchase and from what supplier, with information about discounts and procedures for using designated suppliers.

Questions to ask yourself:

- What suppliers is the franchisor using?
- Have these suppliers had any liquidity issues?
- Do these suppliers have clean track records of providing what they state they provide?

Item 10: Financing

This section provides information on any financing programs the franchisor may extend to franchisees, as well as any relationships that the franchisor has with outside lenders. There may be beneficial programs that the franchisor can help you with. Remember, if the franchisor lends you money to purchase the franchise, it is no different than borrowing from a bank. If you default, the franchisor can terminate your franchise agreement.

Questions to ask yourself:

- Am I sufficiently capitalized to enter into a franchise agreement?
- Am I able to abide by the terms and conditions of the financing?

Item 11: Franchisor's Obligations

This section describes the operational assistance, such as training, advertising, site selection, market research, and computer programs the franchisor provides. This is a very important section, so be sure to read through it carefully. Be particularly alert for qualifying words such as "at our discretion" or "as needed" or "from time to time." These are items that may trip you up later in your franchise life. Remember that these phrases give wide latitude to any subsequent purchaser of the franchise system, and they can be used to change the game. If you are not sure or comfortable with something, be sure to completely understand how it could impact you in the future.

Item 10 also covers how the national advertising fees are handled. This can be a significant amount of money that you are paying into the franchisor's account to be used at the franchisor's discretion. Do the franchisees feel they are getting value from this? Are the franchisees part of the decision-making process around how the franchisor uses the funds? This section merits a conversation with the franchisor to understand how these funds are spent.

This item also outlines the content and scope of the franchisor's support services. It should include disclosures about cash registers and related information involving the use of extremely sensitive franchisee data to which the franchisor has access. Again, watch out for those subtle qualifying words, such as "at our discretion" or "as needed," and know that you may not be able to count on receiving those services. Look carefully to see how much of your required advertising fees actually get spent on advertising, and how much can be siphoned off into uses that mainly benefit the franchisor. Also, note that if franchisees are not involved in managing the national marketing fund and program, it can be a major red flag for investors

Questions to ask yourself:

- Do the services and items the franchisor provides seem reasonable and make sense for your business?
- Can you find examples from your research where what the franchisor states it provides is not what is written?
- Does the section include vague terminology?

Item 12: Territory

This section states how the territory is established (e.g., by square mileage, population, zip codes, etc.), whether it is exclusive, and retention rights of both the franchisee and franchisor to the territory

Questions to ask yourself:

- Is the amount territory I am receiving enough to keep me safe from internal competition?
- Is the territorial protection offered enough to keep other locations from encroaching upon my territory?

Item 13: Trademarks

This section describes all trademarks, trade names, logos, and commercial symbols registered with the U.S. Patent and Trademark Office

Questions to ask yourself:

- What trademarks does the franchisor have, if any, that add value to the franchise?
- How can you quantify this value?
- Do the franchisees say it is valuable?
- Are any of the proprietary symbols set to expire?

Item 14: Patents, Copyrights, and Proprietary Information

This section covers the patents and copyrights owned by the franchisor, and may also describe "business trade secrets."

Questions to ask yourself:

- Are any of these trade secrets "too obvious" to be a secret?
- How valuable are the patents and secrets?
- Are any of the patents and copyrights set to expire?

Item 15: Obligation to Participate in the Actual Operation of the Franchise Business

This section states whether, and to what extent, the franchisee must be personally involved in running the franchise business operations.

Questions to ask yourself:

- Is the level of involvement expected the same as the level of involvement I can contribute?
- Am I ready to contribute more than what is stated in the document?

Item 16: Restrictions on What the Franchisee May Sell

This section includes imposed limits and restrictions on what the franchisee may sell.

Questions to ask yourself:

- Are these restrictions fair?
- Do any of these restrictions stifle your desires as a business owner to the point where you would feel annoyed or hampered in the running of the business?

Item 17: Renewal, Termination, Transfer and Dispute Resolution

This section details all contingencies and options for renewing, terminating, or transferring the business, as well as mediation procedures for settling disagreements between the franchisor and franchisee.

Questions to ask yourself:

- Do all of the specific terms make sense for this section?
- Am I able to hold this entity for a long period of time if I wish to?
- Are there any blatant loopholes or statements that make me uncomfortable about entering into the agreement as a whole?

Item 18: Public Figures

This section describes any endorsement and compensation arrangements with public figures involved in promoting or managing the franchise

Questions to ask yourself:

- Do I respect the figures that have endorsed the product? (At a minimum, you do not need to like them, but you should respect them.)
- Have these figures done anything that has tarnished their reputation that in turn can tarnish the reputation of the company?
- Is the public figure so tied into the image of the company that if the public figure died, it would undermine the ability of the company to continue?

Item 19: Financial Performance Representations

This section includes the actual and projected average earnings of the franchise and how the figures are derived. Some franchisors do not furnish earnings estimates or projections. The best source for this information is from franchisees already in operation. Since, this tends to be the part of the FDD that franchise candidates look at immediately upon receiving the FDD, it merits a closer inspection and thorough comprehension. Fisher Zucker, one of the premier franchise business law firms in the country, has an excellent Web site with significant information about franchise law and states the following:

An earnings claim is defined as "any information from which a specific level or range of actual or potential sales, costs, income or profit from franchised or non-franchised units may be easily ascertained.[1]" If a franchisor makes an earnings claim, in any form, it must be disclosed in Item 19 of the UFOC, and it must meet the detailed disclosure requirements contained in the UFOC guidelines.

Pursuant to the FTC Rule, an earnings claim must have a reasonable basis to support the accuracy of the claim, the documents to substantiate the claim must be in the franchisor's possession, and the claim must be geographically relevant to the prospective location. The FTC Rule requires, in "immediate conjunction with any earnings claim, the disclosure of the number and percentage of the outlets which the franchisor or broker knows to have made at least the same results as those presented in the claim." Franchisee-and company-owned outlets must be reported separately. Finally, all earnings claims must include the following warning in any projection or forecast:

These figures are only estimates; there is no assurance you will do as well. If you rely upon our figures, you must accept the risk of not doing as well.

With regard to the "reasonable basis" of an earnings claim, the American Institute of Certified Public Accountants ("AICPA") publications, which define the "reasonable basis" necessary to support accounting claims, suggest by analogy that the following considerations are relevant:

- The quality of the information.
- Whether the claims are based on the best information available.
- Whether the claims represent the single most probable result.
- The existence of reasonable support for any assumptions.

- Whether the claims are prepared by qualified personnel.
- The accuracy of previous forecasts or projections.

For earnings claims based on past performance, the underlying data must be capable of independent examination and verification and must reasonably support the claim. A franchisor's earnings claim has no reasonable basis if: (1) the results are achieved by a small minority of franchisees; (2) earnings are due to a non-recurring condition; or (3) franchisees use inconsistent methods for reporting earnings.

Questions to ask yourself:

- Are these earnings reasonable?
- Are these earnings what I need for my own personal goals?
- Do I fully understand the data that I am seeing?

Item 20: Outlets and Franchisee Information

This section lists all the franchises ever sold, including those currently in operation, company-owned units, and franchises terminated during the previous three years.

Questions to ask yourself:

- Have there been more franchises opened or closed in the last three years?
- Why have these units closed?
- Is there any information that looks out of place or strange?

Item 21: Financial Statements

Most states require the franchisor to include audited financial statements, including a balance sheet for the past fiscal year, and income statements from the past three fiscal years

Questions to ask yourself:

- Does the national brand have enough reserve capital to cover downturns in the market or PR blunders or any other mishap that could hurt your business through the franchisor being impacted?
- Does the franchisor's income seem sustainable or reasonable?
- Do financial ratios, when conducted on these statements, show a positive trend in the company?

Item 22: Contracts

This section is the actual franchise agreement, which should conform to all the stipulations outlined in the UFOC/FDD. There will be some blanks that must be filled in, and then you will sign the agreement.

Questions to ask yourself:

- Are there any special clauses that I need to be aware of in this area?
- Is there any fine print?

Item 23: Receipt

This section acknowledges that the prospective franchisee has received the UFOC/FDD, but does not obligate the franchisee to sign the agreement.

The Federal Trade Commission does not provide copies of FDDs; however, there are avenues that you can access if you wish to see FDDs without talking with a franchisor. There are three organizations that sell FDDs:

1. FRANdata Corporation
2. FranchiseHelp
3. Franchise-Insider

There are also 3 state government organizations where you can access FDDs that have been filed in that particular state. These are available for free.

1. **Cal-EASI** (Documents not word-searchable)
   California Department of Corporations
   1515 K Street, Suite 200
   Sacramento, CA 95814-4052
   866 ASK-CORP
   http://www.corp.ca.gov/CalEASI/caleasi.asp

2. **OpenFran - The Franchise Openness Project**
   (Documents word searchable)
   PO Box 25514
   Scottsdale, AZ 85255
   480-264-0050
   http://www.openfran.org

3. **Minnesota Department of Commerce**
   85 7th Place East, Suite 500
   St. Paul, MN 55101
   651-296-4026
   https://www.cards.commerce.state.mn.us/CARDS/

"The FDD is an excellent source of information, but never allow it to be your sole source of information. Trust, but verify."

—Joe Dunn, ESQ, Fisher Zucker

CHAPTER 15 - UNDERSTANDING FINANCIAL STATEMENTS

All businesses have a financial framework that they must follow. This chapter will briefly introduce you to the world of financial accounting. This topic *is crucial* to running any business. I will simplify the following parts of financial statements: balance sheet, income statement, and cash flow statement. The other aspects of financial statements are not as crucial for franchisee entities to understand from day one, but those looking to comprehend financial accounting further can look into "notes and disclosures" and "statement of retained earnings." We will be exploring these items through the lens of the fictional company, "Cosmic Cleaners LLC."

Balance Sheet

This is the part of the business model that shows what you have from an aggregate view. Think of this as an up-to-date log of debts, property, and so on—the financial snapshot of the company. This statement is broken up into three parts:

Assets:

This is the stuff you have. Be it cash, property, or money people owe you, all of these things are considered to be aspects of your business that provide you with value.

Liabilities:

These are things that you owe. Whether it is a loan on a car or salaries you owe employees, at one point those things are all liabilities.

Owner's Equity:

Simply put, this is what is left over after you take your assets and pay off all your liabilities. It is what you own in the business and what you have put in. Remember, having money in equity *doesn't mean you draw it out,* but you can *retain it* in the business to reinvest it. If you feel the company needs more money, you can always pay capital (self-financing) to boost what the company has (assets).

Franchisee Implications:

First off, you want to ensure that as the company develops, you have more assets than liabilities. Companies that are in more debt than they can handle, and those that cannot produce enough money to pay off that debt and be profitable will eventually fail. As long as assets outweigh expenses, you likely have a healthy balance sheet.

Basic Formula: Assets = Liabilities + Owner's Equity

Cosmic Cleaners Balance Sheet As of March 2000		
Assets		
Cash	$130,000	
Cleaning Machinery	$500,000	
Cleaning Supplies	$150,000	
	Total Assets	$780,000
Liabilities		
Salary's Due	$75,000	
Bank Loan	$45,000	
Royalty Fees Due	$20,000	
	Total Liabilities	$140,000
Owner's Equity		
Retained Earnings	$110,000	
(-Cash Drawn)	-50,000	
Personal investment or Paid In Capital	$580,000	
	Total Owner's Equity	$640,000
Total Liabilities and Owner's Equity		$780,000

Income Statement

This document is not a big-picture statement, but it describes how a company is doing financially from period to period. A period could be a quarter of a year, a full year, or longer depending on the enterprise. To keep things simple, let us assume that a period is a year. We will discuss the major parts of this statement and what they mean for your business.

Income:

This is all the money you take in. Whether it is sales of a product or a service you provide, the money you make is included in this area of the income statement. Some income statements have different names for this area and further classify things into different sections, but remember that this section represents money earned.

Expenses:

This includes any expense you could possibly have. From salaries to franchise fees, do not forget to put all expenses through this area. Even taxes are expenses that you must account for.

Net Income:

This is the final line item for most income statements. This is income minus expenses. Your profit at the end of your period goes in this section.

Cosmic Cleaners Income Statement From January 1, 2000-January 1, 2001		
Income		
Cleaning Service Revenue	$200,000	
"Healthy Carpet Spray" Can Sales	$55,000	
	Total Sales	$255,000
Expenses		
Salary Expenses	$75,000	
Machinery Maintenance	$10,000	
Cleaning Materials	$15,000	
Healthy Carpet Can Purchases	$25,000	
Franchisor Fees (10% Sales)	$20,000	
	Total Expenses	$145,000
Net Income		$110,000

Franchisee View:

Your entity must strive for positive net income. The goal of a healthy and sustainable enterprise is to ensure that after your expenses are paid, you are creating a surplus. There may be a few periods that produce negative net income during a downturn, but if this persists, your company will fail.

I would advise that you have enough back-up money to handle losses during uncertain times; without safety money, you could go out of business once any disaster strikes. Net income is money that is retained by the business, and you can access it. If you own the company, you own the net income. One of the main reasons businesses fail is that they are undercapitalized and lack staying power through tough times.

Cash Flow Statement

There are multiple approaches to organizing this type of statement, but to keep things simple, let us explore the basic requirements. The cash flow statement's purpose is to show how cash is moving in and out of a business, and it is also expressed in periods. Your personal checkbook is an example of your cash flow statement. A simple example of this type of statement is as follows:

Cosmic Cleaners Cash Flows From January – March, 2000		
Incoming Cash		
Cleaning Services	$150,000*	
Loans	$30,000**	
"Healthy Carpet Spray Can" Sales	$35,000	
	Total Inflow Cash	$215,000
Outgoing Cash		
Salaries	$75,000	
Maintenance	$10,000	
Cleaning Materials	$15,000	
"Healthy Carpet Can Spray" Purchases	$25,000	
Franchisor Royalty Fees	$20,000	
	Total Outflow Cash	$145,000

*All sales or services may not be paid in cash. If they pay in credit, or give you a promise to pay at a later date, you don't recognize the cash until you receive it.

**Notice how money from loans is on the cash flow statement, but not the income statement. This is simply because money from a loan is not income—it is money from a debt.

Franchisee View

This broad overview gives you a chance to dive into some of what to expect when it comes to creating financial models and planning out your business. What has been explained will keep you alive as you figure out how to operate your business from a financial standpoint, but doing more research increases your chances of being successful in the financial arena. There are many nuances that can affect a business from a financial standpoint, and having proper financial statements can sometimes be the difference between getting a loan and being rejected for one. Most quality franchisors assist franchisees in this area by building yearly business plans and then having regular touch points to evaluate where a franchisee is according to that plan, but failure to properly account for things can result in getting in trouble with the government, as well as financial ruin. If you do not feel comfortable with this aspect of a business, hiring an accountant is crucial. In fact, you are probably going to want to have a bookkeeper come in and take care of many of the routine aspects of keeping your books, since you will find it is cheaper and more effective to pay someone to do this instead of your taking time from your business to do it yourself.

Summary

Without a proper financial plan and understanding of accounting, a business can and will fail. The three key statements you must understand from the beginning are balance sheets, income statements, and cash flow statements. Balance sheets show a broad snapshot of a business' position. Income statements show where your money is coming from each period and where it is going. Cash flows follow cash aspect of a business, showing how the cash is travelling from period to period. The last thing you want is failure due to improper planning of your money or not following the rules. If you do not feel able or willing to handle this portion of the business, hire an accountant or pay for a financial consultant. Doing everything yourself is the most expensive thing you can do in business- time is money.

CHAPTER 16 - FINANCING FRANCHISES

It's far better to buy a wonderful company at a fair price than a fair company at a wonderful price.

—Warren Buffett

As you think about which franchise is the best fit, financing the venture is going to be a paramount consideration. How large of an investment into a franchise you can afford and how you are going to finance the franchise are two issues that require investigation. As Buffett wisely states, very often the best option may not be the least expensive. Quality costs money, and like everything else in life, you get what you pay for when purchasing a franchise. While there are many inexpensive options out there, there are always trade-offs, and the franchise that costs $25,000 may very well end up being more expensive in the long run than the one that costs $250,000 initially. This chapter examines how franchises are financed.

If you have purchased a property, you have gone through many of the same steps that it takes to purchase a business. You did an analysis of what you could afford to purchase, what your ability to handle the mortgage payments would be, and were then pre-approved by a lender before you started making offers on properties. Do the same before you dive too deeply into a particular franchise, and your search will be more efficient. Why become enamored of a business that you can't afford to buy? It's the same as going house hunting in a neighborhood of mansions when the house you really require and can afford is a 3 bedroom / 2 bath in a good school district. A difference between buying a business and buying a property is that there are many more avenues to access funds for the purchase of a business than for the purchase of a property.

All of this is predicated, however, on a very simple assumption: that you have some capital and a decent credit score to work with before you decide to own a business. I am continually amazed by people who call my office, have very little educational or professional credentials, and somehow have heard they can open a Waffle House or an I-Hop with no money down based upon government grants. This is not a reality. While the International Franchise Association does have a number of programs that offer tremendous benefits to various groups such as veterans, women, and minorities, in order to own a business, you are going to have to prove you are ready to make a real financial commitment to the endeavor.

There are significant tax benefits and challenges you must understand with all of the options that we will discuss. As a result, it is important to consult with a qualified advisor to understand your best capital structure. Unless you are in the fortunate position to have a bag full of money that you are looking to use to finance a business with, you are going to be analyzing how you will fund your business.

There are specialized franchise funding companies that can work with you to give you a good overview of the various options that you have. I recommend calling them to get an understanding of what they have to offer. There are many institutions out there, but three that have good reputations are:

1. Franfund: www.franfund.com
2. Benetrends: www.benetrends.com
3. Guidant: www.guidantfinancial.com

Any of these companies can do a full personalized analysis of your financial situation and advise you on the benefits or drawbacks of the realistic options that you have available to you.

Whichever route you decide on, there are really two types of funding for your business: other people's money and your money. Oftentimes, it is a combination of both that is the winning formula. Let's take a look at what options are available in both categories.

Other People's Money

There is no such thing as free money. Anytime someone is going to take a risk and loan you money, that person or entity is going to take a look at the Five C's of Credit as they pertain to your situation. Knowing what the five C's are and what your position is will help you get a realistic picture of whether you can access other people's money:

- **Character:** Lenders want to put their money with clients who have solid character.
- **Capacity:** How much debt can the company handle, and what is the borrower's track record of repayment?
- **Capital:** Lenders want to see that the borrower has invested their own money in the business.
- **Conditions:** What are the current economic conditions, and how does the company fit in?
- **Collateral:** Cash flow is the primary source of repayment of a loan, but collateral represents a secondary source.

There are a number of options out there for loans. Here are a few:

Small Business Administration (SBA)

Many people think that the Small Business Administration is an entity that will directly loan them money to start a business. That is not the case. The Small Business Administration is a U.S. government agency that provides support to entrepreneurs and small businesses via state offices and approximately nine hundred small business development centers. SCORE (Service Corps of Retired Executives), are volunteer corps of retired and experienced business leaders who are affiliated with this agency and help entrepreneurs with their businesses. A component of this support is the loan program that the SBA administers. The SBA does not provide grants or direct loans, with the exception of Disaster Relief Loans. Instead, the SBA makes loans through a bank, credit union, or other lenders who partner with the SBA, and the SBA provides a government-backed guarantee on part of the loan against default, so long as the loan conforms to its guidelines. You will typically invest 10-30 percent of your own capital as a "cash injection" into the business in order to qualify for an SBA loan. As an example, if you are looking for a $3,000,000 loan, you would need to invest anywhere from $300,000 to $900,000, depending upon the industry, geographic location, and your credit profile. There are multiple programs that the SBA administers, such as the SLA or Small Loan Advantage program that currently has a maximum loan amount of $350,000 and can be funded much more rapidly than other types of loans.

As these programs are administered by SBA's partners and are not direct loans from SBA, you can call one of the funding companies named earlier and the company will work with you to put together an SBA loan application and then shop it to a wide number of SBA-approved lenders throughout the United States in order to find the best rate. Should you wish to consult a local lender and discuss your loan proposal with one of their loan officers, you can find a list of SBA-approved lenders by calling your state SBA office. When meeting with the lender, be prepared to discuss your proposal in detail. You should have the following available for the lenders review: your business plan, your personal financial statements, your business financial statements (if already a business), collateral available to secure the loan, assumptions used in your projected earnings statements, management resumes of those involved in operating the business, and pro-forma balance sheets showing what the business would look like if the loan were granted. The lender may also request that you schedule a face-to-face interview to discuss the business in greater detail.

An SBA loan typically has a repayment term between five and twenty-five years depending on the life of the assets being financed.

Frandata is a website that compiles The SBA Franchise Registry, which is a national listing of franchise systems whose franchisees receive expedited loan processing when applying for financial assistance from the U.S. Small Business Administration. This is because particular franchise systems have been pre-approved by the SBA. This shows that the franchisor is working to make your process more efficient and should be viewed positively. It also shows that the SBA has experience in lending to this system, and that should cut down on some of the red tape.

The SBA Web site has a wealth of information on many funding options.

Bank Loan

The main difference between an SBA-facilitated loan and a loan through a bank is essentially the lender's risk factor. Because giving loans to start-up companies can be risky business, the government has intervened to stimulate lending to start-ups, guaranteeing a portion of the loan to the bank. This guarantee means that if a business goes downhill and is incapable of paying its principle, the government will repay a percentage of the default.

Banks may lend on existing businesses that they know. If you are purchasing an existing business, you may want to speak with the previous owner's banker. They may know the business well enough to be comfortable in loaning you money to facilitate the purchase. You may also have a good relationship with your local bank that merits a call to the local banker to talk about options the bank may be able to offer you.

Home Equity Line of Credit

A Home Equity Line of Credit ("HELOC") is often used to purchase a business since it has a lower interest rate than an SBA loan and can be attained quickly, provided you have equity in your home. If you are contemplating owning a business, my recommendation is to get a HELOC prior to quitting your job. You will find it much easier to get a HELOC if you are employed than if you are self-employed.

Securities-Based Lending

A securities-based loan is conceptually very similar to a margin loan, or lending that is collateralized by the securities in your stock account. However, there are some significant differences between this type of loan and a true margin loan. A margin loan is known as "purpose credit" because the purpose of the credit is to purchase more stocks, and there is a limit on borrowing set to 50 percent of the value of the stock or other securities being margined. The primary purpose of a margin loan is for an investor to use margin credit to purchase more stock. A securities-based lending account is a "non-purpose" credit structure, meaning that more than 50 percent of the stock or portfolio's value can be lent, provided that the proceeds are not used to purchase marginable securities. This is the critical difference.

1. Securities-based credit lines are technically variable rate interest-only loans with no set maturity date. There is no penalty for early payoff, and rates are typically 1%-3% lower than with fixed-rate loans.

2. Securities-based fixed-rate loans are term loans usually between 1 and 7 years. An early payoff penalty may be assessed depending on the length (term) of the loan and the time remaining to maturity

You keep the securities in your account subject to several restrictions. For instance, you cannot trade these securities multiple times in one day, or make block trades (trades over $250,000). Just as you would be with a traditional margin account, you will be subject to a "house call" if the value of your portfolio falls below a certain percentage. This type of funding can be achieved very rapidly since you have collateral to ensure the loan amount in the form of your stock.

Equipment Loans/Leases

One third of all equipment in the U.S. is leased. There are many options in franchising for obtaining loans collateralized by the underlying equipment. If you think of the many different pieces of equipment that various franchise concepts require, you have a variety of options. From vehicles to restoration equipment, water mitigation units to pizza ovens, many franchise concepts require physical equipment to make the franchise work. There is a robust and well-established field of lending and leasing equipment, and if your franchise requires equipment, the franchisor should have programs they have negotiated to help you with the purchase or lease of equipment.

Crowdfunding

Younger entrepreneurs ask me about crowdfunding options, whereby funds are solicited from online investors. It is an option that merits understanding since it has attracted significant attention, not only in the media but also from policymakers. In fact, crowdfunding was recently mentioned in the Jumpstart Our Business Startups (JOBS) Act, which was signed into law in 2012. While this is an interesting field that is growing rapidly, I have not seen any franchisees fund themselves this way.

Friends/Family

According to Kirk Neiswander, senior vice president of Enterprise Development Inc., a nonprofit subsidiary of Case Western Reserve University's Weatherhead School of Management in Cleveland, "Family are not reckless investors, and they have shallow pockets. They will invest once but not a second or a third time and generally in an industry they know that is close to home. Typically, friends and family will invest up to $100,000."

Friends and family present a formidable source of capital. Your typical friend or family investor is male, has been successful in his own business, and wants to invest because he wishes someone had done it for him.

However, investments with friends and family can have negative consequences if things don't go as planned. The situation can be even worse than with professional investors because friends and family react to bad news with added emotion. Take the following steps to provide adequate protection for everyone:

1. Get an agreement in writing. This will eliminate all conversations that start with, "You never said that."

2. Emphasize debt (loans) rather than equity (ownership). You don't want friends and family to be involved in your company forever. Before you know it, they will start telling you how to run the place, and long-buried emotions will emerge. Limit their involvement to the loan, and pay it back as fast as you can.

3. Put some cash flow on their investment. If Dad says, "Here's $50,000—try not to lose it, and pay it back as soon as you can," that's great. But consider paying some nominal interest at regular intervals to provide you both with a reality check. And it's better to pay this interest quarterly rather than monthly. This way,

190

when things are teetering, your lender won't immediately know it.

Angel Investments

Angel investors are individuals who will personally fund companies that they believe in. They are not professional investors. Their funding comes in at very early stages, and they usually invest less than $100,000. They will almost certainly require some debt or ownership stake in the company, and they may or may not want a seat on the company's board of directors. Some angels work together in networks, but the premise is the same. Make sure you understand all the terms you are agreeing to if you choose this option.

Venture Capitalists

These are professional investors who make it their job to invest in companies. They will invest into your idea, and they will make it a priority to have a seat on your board. They will usually take a significant ownership interest and will require in- depth information before they invest.

Grants/Prizes

If you achieve funding for a franchise using a grant or a prize, please call or e-mail me! This form of funding is really dependent on your technology or how you can positively impact a community, whether locally or on a larger scale. If you are developing a franchise that is supported by government or non-governmental organization (NGO) funding (green energy for example), or if your franchise fulfills a community need, you may be able to find grant money. This is money that you can use for purposes that the grant guidelines define. The government or NGO will take no ownership interest. Beyond grants, there are a number of entrepreneurial contests and incubators throughout the United States. Applying for and winning these competitions and grants might result in some funding for a start-up franchise. Don't spend a lot of time investigating this category. It is highly unlikely that you will receive a grant or a prize to purchase the franchise you are interested in.

There are a myriad of options to find money in this country. There are countless stories of entrepreneurs using everything from credit cards to precious art work to fund ventures. Just remember the number one rule when using other people's money: other people want their money back at some point... with interest!

Your Money

A bank is a place that will lend you money if you prove you don't need it.

—Bob Hope

The past few years have had a significant impact on the type of funding mechanisms that franchise buyers utilize. Loans have been harder to obtain, and with a significant percentage of the population of entrepreneurs coming from the ranks of senior management, there has been an increase in self-funding options.

Cash

Though you may have bundles of cash just lying around waiting to be deployed, take a closer look at the tax implications before doing so. It may be that there are other options that are more beneficial. Regardless, if you purchase your business yourself with cash, it is completely yours. You control every aspect of it. For some individuals, this is a comfort that is important.

Rollover as Business Start-Up

Call them accidental entrepreneurs, unintended entrepreneurs, forced entrepreneurs, or just entrepreneurs, but many franchise buyers are corporate refugees who are fending for themselves after coming to the realization that they are not going to find another management position anytime soon. Very often, these entrepreneurs hold significant assets in their retirement accounts and are often surprised to hear that they can access these funds to start a business. This has become a very popular way to fund a new venture, since 401(K) assets and their appreciation are not taxed, and if you can access these funds tax and penalty free, it can provide you with significant buying power.

There are explicit exemptions in both Tax and ERISA law that were created to encourage investment in small business – the backbone of America's economy. There is a process where an individual can invest up to one hundred percent of their eligible retirement assets into a franchise. The program is called Rollovers for Business Startups (ROBS). Started in the 1970s, the goal of the program is to allow people to pull money from their retirement accounts without tax or penalty to invest in a business start-up. Basically what you're doing is creating a corporation that has a 401(K) plan, then rolling old 401(K) assets that have been rolled over into an IRA into the new company's 401(K) plan. You are then selling the assets in your old 401(K) / IRA and buying stock issued by the new corporation. You can then use the cash generated from the sale of the assets to purchase a franchise.

Rollover Business Startup

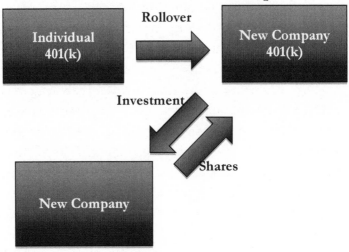

A rollover start-up plan consists of four steps:

1. Form a C Corporation (this is a requirement for this plan)
2. This Corporation sponsors a 401(K) plan
3. You, as an employee of the corporation, roll over retirement monies into the new 401(K) plan.
4. The new 401(K) plan invests in the corporation.

This method can be a good way to fund your new venture since you have no debt, have an ongoing employee benefit in the form of a 401(K) plan and are investing into yourself. However, if you ask your financial advisor what he or she thinks, you are likely to get an earful that includes words like "illegal" or "suspect" or "dangerous." Typically, financial advisors are against these types of plans because they entail you moving your money away from the advisor, and the advisor is probably paid a fee for "managing your money." A client once told me that he decided he would rather manage his own money than have someone else manage it and that the investment he trusted the most was himself.

This is a sophisticated way to fund a business, but there are many possible pitfalls. You want to make sure you are working with a firm that has experience in, and routinely handles a large volume of, these types of transactions. Your CPA probably doesn't have experience with these types of transactions, so be sure to use a reputable firm that specializes in this type of planning. The plan and its operations must conform to the requirements of Section 401(a) of the IRC. The purchase of common stock of a "Plan Sponsor" by the Plan Sponsor's retirement plan is exempt from the prohibited transaction rules under Section 4975(d)(13) of the IRC and Section 408(e) of ERISA if: (1) the purchase is for adequate consideration, (2) no commission is charged, and (3) the purchasing plan is an eligible individual account plan as defined in section 407(d)(3) of ERISA. The IRS has spent a considerable amount of time in its review of this type of transaction and has reached the following conclusion: "We do not believe the form of these transactions may be challenged as non-compliant." When the Employee Retirement Income Security Act was passed in 1974, it allowed people to invest their 401(K) or other plan monies into stock within their own businesses. Some of the firms that perform this type of transaction are designated by the IRS as "Volume Submitters." This grants these firms a blanket determination letter that covers the 401(K) Profit Sharing Plans that they create and also provides for ongoing monitoring of the program to protect against any future issues that may cost you taxes or penalties.

The International Franchise Association is constantly working to promote business ownership throughout the United States. By empowering groups that might not have had the opportunity to join the ranks of successful business owners, the IFA has helped thousands attain business ownership. There are a number of programs that are worthy of mention:

VetFran

VetFran was born out of the desire of the late Don Dwyer Sr., founder of The Dwyer Group, in appreciation of our country's veterans. To carry forward this noble mission, his daughter and past IFA Chair, Dina Dwyer-Owens, has worked tirelessly to honor the men and women who have served their country. VetFran members commit to offering financial incentives to franchisees that meet their requirements. Since each franchise system is different, each franchisor decides how to structure its own VetFran offering. Some franchisors provide financial incentives by reducing their initial franchise or other fees or by contributing to the franchisee's initial cost of investment.

The IFA and its members receive no government funding for VetFran, and the program is entirely voluntary. Participating is as much an honor to the franchisor as it is honoring the service of our veterans.

VetFran's ranks have grown to include more than five hundred franchise systems that voluntarily offer financial incentives to veterans seeking to become franchise small-business owners. Through the VetFran program, thousands of servicemen and women have become business owners.

MinorityFran

The mission of the IFA Educational Foundation's Diversity Institute is to increase the number and success of minorities in franchising, including franchisors, franchisees, suppliers, and employees. The initiative builds on relationships forged with leading organizations through the IFA Diversity Institute, such as the National Urban League, the Association of Small Business Development Centers, the Minority Business Development Agency, the U.S. Hispanic Chamber of Commerce, the National Black MBA Association, and the Minority Business Development Agency. The goal is not only to increase the numbers of minority franchisees but to send a message to all communities that franchising is a smart way to realize the American dream of small-business ownership. Each franchise system that participates in this program structures their support differently, so you will want to ask the franchise companies directly if they participate in this program and what their structure looks like.

Funding a Franchise

Financing a business doesn't mean you have all the money in the world, it means you know the best strategies to achieve your aim. We are franchise people in the money business, rather than the other way around.

—Geoffery Seiber, CEO of FranFund

Finances are unique to the individual.

—Rocco Fiorentino, CEO of Benetrends

How you finance the business is almost as important as the business concept itself. A key reason that businesses fail is a lack of capital from the start.

—David Nilssen, CEO of Guidant Financial

One of the greatest resources we have in this country is the capital markets. The ability to align capital with ideas has made this country what it is and has given countless entrepreneurs the ability to change their world. America is a financially sophisticated country with a wide menu of financial products to choose from in any situation. Financing a start-up entity will present you with a variety of options. There are organizations that will help you to understand your options and work with you to help you achieve funding. Ultimately, make sure that your funding matches up with your capabilities and goals.

CHAPTER 17 - BUSINESS STRUCTURE

The competitor to be feared is one who never bothers about you at all, but goes on making his own business better all the time.

—*Henry Ford*

Deciding how to incorporate and run your business are not choices that should be made lightly. The foundations you are building for your company determine how far you can take your business in the long run.

Choosing a corporate structure is a highly personalized endeavor that allows the entrepreneur to reduce liability, minimize taxes, and ensure that the business survives. It allows the business owner to create an entity that will prosper, even after the owner is long gone. Since there are three different types of corporate structures that you can choose; C-Corp, S-Corp and LLC, it is important to think about the corporation and then incorporate under the structure that is most beneficial to your aims. Think about what you are trying to achieve with the following:

1. To what degree are your personal assets at risk from liabilities that may arise from your business?
2. What tax advantages do you consider the most important?

3. Will you want to bring investors, at present or in the future, into the business?

4. Will you want to grant ownership to future employees?

While these are important aspects to your corporation, there is a lot more to a corporation than most people are aware of. Educating yourself is the first step.

Business in America

America is the most litigious society in the world with a lawsuit being filed every two seconds. Incorporating will not only help you protect your assets but also give you a wealth of tangible benefits that most people are not aware of. One of the first things you will want to do when considering owning a franchise is to learn about corporate structure and what will be the best option for you. You will want to obtain a CPA or tax professional's advice before you incorporate in order to understand these structures and how they will impact you. A good place to start is the American Institute of Certified Public Accounts, or AICPA. If you don't have a CPA or tax professional, you can call the Chamber of Commerce in your town and ask for three referrals of qualified professionals who work with small businesses. Let's take a moment to view the general benefits of business ownership, and then examine specific classes of businesses.

General Benefits of Business Incorporation

Limited Liability for Shareholders

Since a corporation is a legal entity, it is separate from the officers, shareholders, and owners. This means that the law specifically provides for protection of personal assets if there are corporate obligations that cannot be met. When you create a corporation, you create an entity that can own property, enter into contracts, pay taxes, and sue and be sued independently of the people who own the corporation. However, there is a caveat: the corporation's assets and liabilities must be completely separate from the shareholders' assets and responsibilities. The simplest way to do this is to have a professional set up your corporation and make sure that the business and the person or people who own it do not commingle funds or assume liabilities for each other. Practically, the corporation must have its own checking account, credit cards, and debt. If the corporation is not properly structured, you risk the "corporate veil" being pierced, and that can put your personal assets at risk.

Raising Capital

If you are planning on raising capital, either through debt or equity, a corporation offers significant advantages and flexibility. There are multiple types of stock that can be sold, such as nonvoting shares, which gives a shareholder the right to receive a profit distribution but not have control over business activity. This allows the corporation's owners to raise money while maintaining the freedom to make business decisions without others' input or consent.

Flexibility of Ownership

Of the major corporation types, a C corporation offers significant flexibility in ownership. Shares can be owned by individuals, other companies, trusts, partnerships, or other entities. This allows the business the ability to create capital partnerships with entities that other types of structures cannot.

Fiscal Year/Income Splitting

What date is the end of your year? If, like most people, you said December 31, you are partially right. Individuals, S Corporations, and LLCs typically have their fiscal year ending on December 31. However, a C corporation can choose when it's tax year ends. For example, you may decide that your corporate tax year ends on March 31. This gives you significant ability to split your income across two calendar years. This delays the tax liability on a portion of your income. As an example, let's say you are a shareholder of a C corporation, and it is December 26. You have had a good year, and there is $100,000 worth of capital in the corporation. You can elect to pay yourself $50,000 during the current year and then pay yourself the remaining $50,000 on January 1. The taxes on the first $50,000 will be due on April 15, and the taxes on the second $50,000 will be due on April 15 of the following year. You have effectively delayed your personal tax liability by over fifteen months on the second installment while the entire $100,000 is considered a tax deduction to the corporation since it was paid as salary to an employee. You can only accomplish this method of taxation if your corporate fiscal year ends on a date other than December 31. You will want to consult a tax professional or CPA in order to structure your fiscal calendar effectively.

Perpetual Duration

People die. Corporations can live forever, as long as they are maintained and operated properly. The oldest corporation in the world, until 2006 when it was purchased by another corporation, was Kongo Gumi, a Japanese construction company founded in AD 578. They built Buddhist temples. There's a good lesson here—find a business that has a constant demand, and you have the ability to create something that will outlast you and potentially provide for generations of your family. As of the writing of this book, there were 5,586 companies in the world that are two hundred years old or older. Start the foundations of your legacy properly, and your legacy has the potential to shine through the ages.

Corporate Deductions

There are different deductions that corporations can take, so it is important that you are aware of them. For instance, employee benefits, such as health plans, medical reimbursement, college funding, key man insurance and other benefits are deductible through a C corporation or S corporation but not through an LLC. This can be a significant benefit. The range of corporate deductions is staggering when compared to personal deductions. Be sure to have a CPA advise you on which benefits are pertinent to your personal situation.

Credibility

Just as many people scoff at a non-business e-mail, low-quality business cards, or an "office phone" that is picked up by a child, many will look down upon an entity that is not properly incorporated. You gain credibility by having a true business structure and will be amazed at how many questions you have about what type of incorporation you chose and why by other business professionals. The credibility you instantly gain by being competent to hold a conversation on incorporation strategies is a testament to the professionalism of the business.

Transferability of Ownership

You can sell or transfer a corporately owned business very easily. You can sell a portion or all of it through shares, providing you with significant options when thinking about generational transfers.

Central Management and Corporate Structure

Since corporations have been around for hundreds of years, there is a vast body of knowledge around how to best structure the business. Shareholders, who are the true owners of the business, vote to elect a board of directors. This board of directors is then responsible for overseeing the implementation of the wishes of the owners. The board of directors hires the corporate officers, who then run the daily operations of the business, including hiring employees. Each of these corporate actors is governed by regulations that you can easily replicate. If you find it easier to follow a recipe than to create something from scratch, forming a corporation is going to make a lot of sense!

Lower IRS Audit Probability

The IRS is a noble entity and performs a very important function in the United States. The number one category of audits the IRS performs is on wealthy individuals who are deducting business expenses on their personal tax returns. The 2011 IRS Data Book shows there was an increase across all income levels for audits. With over forty-seven thousand employees in the audit department at the IRS, there is significant oversight. Create the right structure and follow the rules. Remember, Al Capone went to jail for cheating on his taxes! There is a wealth of information out there on how to lower your IRS audit probability, and if you set up a corporation and have a team of professionals working with you on your taxes and structure, you have already taken major strides towards doing so.

Asset Protection

You can think of a corporation as a giant umbrella to keep you dry and protected. A corporation is an excellent vehicle to protect your assets. Know the tools that you have at your disposal and what you are trying to achieve, and a corporation becomes an excellent planning tool for you to use in many aspects of your business life.

You will want to speak with your advisors regarding what the best type of corporate structure is to help you with your specific situation and goals. This chapter will focus on providing a basic overview of four major business structures and some of the financial benefits incorporating may have on your personal situation.

One of the biggest learning moments that many people who have never owned a business have is in understanding how to handle expenses, salary, and owner's benefits. For additional information, an excellent read is *Loopholes of the Rich* by Diane Kennedy.

Learning how a business owner benefits from a business is one of the most important aspects of owning a business. How business owners benefit from their businesses is a function of how they treat their corporations. As an employee, you earn a salary. Think of this as the "above-the-tax-line" or "pretax" number. Taxes are deducted from the gross salary first, leaving you with your take-home, bi-weekly check. Think of this as your "below-the-tax-line" or "post-tax" number. You pay for your living expenses, such as your mortgage, your car, your cell phone, eating out, and entertaining, from your post-tax income. There are very limited deductions that an employee can take from the above-the-tax-line number. Items such as your 401(K) contribution and your health savings account (HSA) come from pretax.

Taxes for business owners differ significantly from employee income taxes. Since the business owner controls the profit and loss items in the business, let's take a look at how a business owner realizes benefits from the corporation.

Profit and Loss Examination

As an example, let's take a look at the expenses of a small business. Bob owns an interior design business; he has no full-time employees other than himself and works from home. Bob built a good team of advisors, including a skilled CPA. The following chart shows the basic financial information for Bob's business.

Gross Income	$500,000
Expenses	
Labor	$200,000
Marketing	$60,000
Communication	$7,500
Auto	$30,000
Travel and Meetings	$60,000
Daycare	$500
Materials	$100,000
Franchise Fees	$50,000
General Maintenance	$10,000
Total Expenses	$518,000
Net Profit (Loss)	($18,000)

It looks like this business lost $18,000 overall. If you have never owned a business or are not familiar with how business owners benefit from a business, you might conclude that this is probably not a good opportunity. If you asked Bob, "How much did your business make last year?" and he said, "It lost $18,000," that would likely turn you off from investing in his business. If you asked a second question, such as "Did you pay yourself?" and he said, "I paid myself $50,000, and I hired my kids to do some stuff," you might be further tempted to shake your head at Bob. Well, at least Bob didn't have to pay any taxes on his corporation, since it didn't make any money.

Our next step helps us understand what expenses are incurred that benefited Bob. Remember, expenses are deductible from business income, lowering the tax burden.

Owner Perks	
Owners Salary	$50,000
Cell Phone Bills (Business Meetings)	$500
Business Travel (Car and Plane)	$23,000
Car Purchase for Work	$30,000
Child Care	$500
Gasoline	$1000
401(k) Investment	$40,000
Total Benefits	$145,000

The reality here is that Bob is not fiddling while his empire is burning; he is actively using his knowledge of his corporation's expenses and legal structure to control his tax liability. He is paying himself $50,000 a year, putting $40,000 into his retirement account. He is also enjoying the benefits of tens of thousands of possible business-related expenses. What are some of those benefits? When he had to travel to Europe to do a study of architecture or drapery treatments in Versailles in order to reproduce them in his interior design business, he claimed that as a business expense. If he took his wife and some prospective clients out to dinner or had an employee function such as a birthday party at a restaurant- that also became a business expense. Certainly he has to drive a car, have a cell phone, a computer, iPad and Internet access to conduct business. Corporations are consumers of products and services just like individuals are. When the individual is an owner or majority shareholder of the business, very often these consumables also benefit them.

Specific Business Entities

Sole Proprietorship

Formation

This is the simplest business to start, as it requires barely any effort. The only possible legal expense would be the acquisition of permits or licenses if your business has such restrictions. If your work does not require any permits, your formation is already complete.

Advantages

1. A sole proprietorship is by far the cheapest business entity to form. Legal consulting may not even be required and permit costs are minimal.
2. You are the sole owner, and thus have 100 percent control. There is absolutely no one to answer to and very few rules from a structural standpoint.
3. The tax preparation is simple and similar to filing your own taxes.

Disadvantages

1. All liabilities are personal liabilities. If your business fails, your personal bank account and all your assets can be targeted. Even employee wrongdoings will be your burden to bear.
2. It is nearly impossible to raise money for a sole proprietorship.

Partnerships - General & Limited

Formation

These entities are created via state registration. The process involves minimal paperwork, and the entity constitutes an association of two or more people. General partners are viewed as full investors, and all personal liabilities the company has fall on the partners. Limited partners are only liable for what they invest in the entity, but they will receive a share of the profits from earnings.

Taxation
Partnerships are flow-through entities, meaning only income distributed to owners is taxed. In effect there is no double taxation.

Advantages
1. No double taxation
2. Limited liability partners have their personal assets protected

Disadvantages
1. General partners assume personal liability of all debts incurred by company
2. All partners must agree when making decisions, as there are not special "share" classifications
3. Limited partners cannot work for the management of the company, though they may do consulting and help in auxiliary ways.

S Corporation

Formation
You will need to submit state and federal paperwork at a minimum, including a 2553 S form with the IRS. The following conditions are from the IRS, and they must be met to obtain S corporation status:
1. Be a domestic corporation that is made in the United States of America

2. Have only allowable shareholders, which include individuals, certain trusts, and estates. No partnerships, other corporations, or non-resident aliens can have shares in the company

3. Have 100 or less shareholders that have shares in the company

4. Every share is worth the same amount and has the same rights. You can't give out special shares.

5. The IRS has to approve you, and you may not have foreign citizens own it.

Taxation

S corporations are what are known as pass-through entities. Think of this as a giant funnel that income and expenses are poured into and whatever ends up, be it a profit or a loss, flows through and drips out of the end of the funnel. No income tax is paid at a federal level, and all business profits pass into the owner's personal tax return. Taxes are paid by the individual, not by the corporate entity at the individual's rate. If the business incurs a loss, that loss will also drip out of the end of the funnel and be deducted from the individuals other income, if any.

Advantages

1. There is no double taxation.

2. The corporation is a completely separate entity from its owner.

3. Ownership is easily transferable.

4. It is easier to take advantage of fringe benefits like medical plans, life insurance, etc.

Disadvantages

1. Shareholders are limited to one hundred in total and must be citizens or permanent residents

2. No further classification of shareholders can be created, making it difficult to use special shares to attract investors.

3. These entities have stricter rules for how a corporation is set up.

C Corporation

Formation
The requisite forms must be submitted to the secretary of state, including a fee. These forms include the submission of bylaws and incorporation documents. A board of directors must be formed and hold a meeting.

Taxation
Think of a C Corporation like a giant bucket. Income and expenses go in and whatever is left over, be it a profit or a loss, is treated as such. Taxation for these entities is a bit more complicated than other corporations as taxes are paid twice: first, on the profit the entity makes as a corporation, and secondly on the distribution to the shareholders be it in the form of salary or a dividend. This is why C Corporations are commonly referred to as "double taxed" entities. If there is a loss to the corporation, the loss resides within the corporation and can be applied to offset future profits.

Advantages
1. The company itself is liable for company actions, not the individual.

2. The board carries on the company business, rather than the owner, allowing for a longer life span for the company, as multiple board members are running the show.

3.   A C corporation is a very well-understood corporate structure with a large body of precedents. Investors are comfortable with this structure and that can lead to a willingness by investors to invest into a business incorporated in this manner. This structure is common with publicly traded companies and large entities.

Disadvantages

1.   A C corporation can have complex financial and legal implications. You will need professionals to handle this structure if you are not well versed in its requirements and ramifications.

2.   Taxes are levied on salary or dividends paid to employees as well as profits that the corporation may earn.

Limited Liability Corporations

Formation

Limited liability entities are created at the state level and thus have differing rules from state to state. These entities cannot be banks or insurance companies, but their owners can be almost anyone else, from individuals to corporations. There is no cap on the number of members, and some states allow "single member" LLCs.

Taxation

These entities operate in a manner similar to S corporations when it comes to taxation; however, unlike S corporations, an LLC is sometimes subject to restrictions regarding paying a salary in cases of self-employment. Beyond that, the tax structure is the same.

Advantages

1. An LLC can be set up very rapidly and inexpensively.
2. This entity allows for an unlimited number of shareholders with an allowance for preferred shares.
3. There is no double taxation, and it is a pass-through entity, like an S corporation.
4. Management has more flexibility to run their business as they wish. There are less rules for set-up than a S-Corp.
5. Company is separate from individual in terms of liabilities.

Disadvantages

1. LLCs are not as prominent as C corporations, which may make obtaining funding more difficult than a C corporation

C Corporations Versus S Corporations Versus LLCs

Differences

1. A C Corporation is a separate entity from the individual and is treated like a separate taxpayer. If profits are distributed as dividends, the owners will pay personal income tax on the distribution. This "double taxation" (profits are first taxed at the corporate level and then at the personal level as dividends) causes many business owners to opt for other forms of incorporation.
2. S Corporations pass profits and losses through to your personal tax return and the S Corporation does not pay taxes.
3. An LLC treats income and losses similar to an S Corp. The LLC has owners and often managers who run the business. The LLC can delegate individuals to run a business.

4. S Corps have directors. These individuals make major decisions regarding the company, and elect officers to run the company.

5. S Corporations are always perpetual- or live forever barring any event that forces it to shut down. Some states make their LLC's have a dissolution date.

6. S Corp transfer of ownership tends to be easier as long as IRS restrictions are met. For LLCs, this transfer typically requires approval from all members of the LLC.

7. LLCs allow almost anyone to be shareholders, from other companies to foreign individuals. S Corps have more restrictions on this matter.

The Bottom Line

Which business structure you choose really comes down to your preferences and your financial aspirations. Any of these structures can support a franchise; most franchisors will work with whichever structure you choose. After all, you are the one paying them to use their business model. One can determine which model is the most effective by bearing personal goals and the various legal and financial ramifications in mind.

Summary

Understanding the broader benefits of business ownership will help you during the implementation process. Purchasing a franchise should include the act of forming a corporation. The S Corp and LLC models tend to be the most common forms franchisees choose, as they minimize personal liabilities and entail a single-taxation approach. The sole proprietorship model is possibly the worst business model for a franchise, or any other business endeavor, with all risk falling on your shoulders. Legal and financial advice from experts and franchise consultants can prove invaluable in navigating this process, as these experts understand the nuances of various business structures and the industry of business operation.

EPILOGUE

Mark decided on a franchise and signed the agreements. He hired a lawyer who set up a corporation for his new venture, went to training, and got his business started. Within a year, he had served over one hundred customers, and many of them turned into repeat business. He followed the franchisor's advice of getting two clients a week. It was amazing to see his company grow right in front of him. He hired more employees and got an accountant on board to make sure all of his franchise financials were in order.

His company was eventually featured in a local magazine, and that publicity only served to increase his customer base. It got to the point where he started to focus most of his efforts on running the company and thinking about future growth. All of this success was thanks to his drive and the franchise company's system.

As the business flourished, he was able to put money aside. He became well versed in the aspects of owning a corporation. He hired his children to do work at the company and they started learning financial lessons that he wished he had learned at their age. He created a college funding plan for his employees that his children, as employees of the company, were able to take advantage of and he was able to fund a portion of their college through the business. He had a strong matching feature on his companies 401(K) and profit sharing plan since part of his exit strategy was to give equity to his loyal employees and one day sell them the business. He was proud to see his family grow stronger month after month, and his franchise had begun to run more efficiently and independently. He didn't have to supervise his employees all the time. Mark spent this extra time away from work with his family on vacations that they looked forward to and remembered long afterwards.

Years later, a moment of true joy came from one unforgettable experience. While walking among one of the smaller rivers near Green Lake Park, his family noticed a small pond across the river among the trees. A man-made path made of flat stones was the only way across the water. Carefully, his family walked across the river. The pond water on the other side remained still and clear, reflecting his family back up at him. Smiling, Mark realized that he had found the steady vision he had been looking for. The blurry, flowing river from his past was gone—the peace he had found came from knowing that what he valued the most was secure: his family. He had achieved his goals through franchising; an endeavor he was grateful he had the courage to undertake.

All our dreams can come true…if we have the courage to pursue them.

—Walt Disney

We have completed a journey together through your reading of this book. Perhaps you have now started another journey in your thoughts and actions towards learning about owning a franchise. Perhaps the culmination of this journey will be in your owning a franchise.

Many of the people who have read this book will not own a franchise. There are far more people who will have dreams of achieving business ownership and the freedom that goes along with it than those who actually make the decision to go for it. You probably already know which one you are.

I believe that we all have the capacity for greatness in whichever form we choose. Making the leap from the known to the unknown is not for the faint of heart. However, once you make that leap, you will wonder why you didn't do it sooner. If you have faith in your ability to overcome obstacles, you will find that you will overcome those obstacles. The fact that you are here today is proof that you come from a long line of ancestors who have overcome tremendous obstacles.

Independence of thought and the ability to enjoy life is something that we all strive for. Whether it is as a student, employee or business owner. Our time on this earth is short. It has been my goal to produce a framework that will save you time and help you in your understanding how to go about evaluating a franchise.

Not all franchise companies are created equal. Some franchisors are merely playing along at being in the franchise business. Perhaps they had a few businesses that worked for them and they have dreams of growing their enterprise upon your back. Some franchisors are little more than a collection of brochures, a logo and seemingly friendly people at the corporate office equipped with ready answers. The franchisees who have bought into these systems oftentimes find themselves facing dire consequences when the reality in the field doesn't match up to the slick ad campaigns. Sadly, these franchisors cast darkness over this noble endeavor and hurt people's lives.

It has been my intention in writing this book to help you understand how to find the right partner in a franchise system. The world is full of people who are fundamentally good. There are visionary, wonderful people out there who have created a replicable business model that will aid you in your quest. You can wrap their experience and support around your desires and have a vehicle that will take you through the challenges of business start-up and beyond. Just as you are looking for the right partner, these franchisors are doing the same thing. They are looking for you.

Like two people finding love in life, if you stay positive and are honest with yourself while you conduct your search, you will find the right partner in the right franchisor. I hope I was able to bring some clarity into this process and equip you with the tools and vision to find and evaluate your ideal franchise partner.

May you look over the horizon and see the path to the life of your dreams.

I wish you the very best of luck in your journey.

If I can be of any assistance to you whatsoever as you contemplate your journey, please do not hesitate to contact me.

800-321-6072

<u>info@TheFranchiseMBA.com</u>

The credit belongs to the man who is actually in the arena; whose face is marred by sweat and blood; who strives valiantly; who errs and comes short again and again because there is no effort without error and shortcoming; who knows the great enthusiasms, the great devotion, spends himself in a worthy cause; who at best knows in the end the triumph of high achievement; and who at worst, if he fails, at least fails while daring greatly, so that his place shall never be with those cold and timid souls who have never tasted victory or defeat.

—Theodore Roosevelt

Your time is limited, so don't waste it living someone else's life. Don't be trapped by dogma – which is living with the results of other people's thinking. Don't let the noise of other's opinions drown out your own inner voice. And most important, have the courage to follow your heart and intuition. They somehow already know what you truly want to become. Everything else is secondary.

—Steve Jobs

ABOUT THE AUTHORS

NICK NEONAKIS

Mr. Neonakis is proof of the American Dream in action; His family moved to the US from Greece when he was a boy and achieved success in this country through hard work and education. His greatest joy - outside of his family - is in helping those who have made the decision to achieve independence through business ownership make their own dream a reality.

Mr. Neonakis' academic credentials include a M.B.A. in Finance, Marketing and Strategy from Case Western Reserve University in Cleveland, OH, a Bachelor of Arts in Economics from Trinity College in Hartford, CT and a degree from the Albert Ludwigs Universitat in Freiburg, Germany. In addition, he has taken numerous post-graduate courses in business, strategy and management. He speaks English and Greek and is comfortable in Spanish, French and German. He guest lectures on the topic of franchising at the Weatherhead School of Management and has been interviewed in several publications.

In addition to his franchise experience, Neonakis has operated a small business in Santorini, Greece and has worked as financial advisor for Morgan Stanley and Charles Schwab in New York City - where he worked at the World Trade Center.

His franchise credentials include being a Vice President of two brands of the largest publicly traded North American franchisor of property services - The Franchise Company / FS Brands division of First Service. This multi-line company is the owner of franchised brands such as California Closets, Paul Davis Restoration, College Pro Painters, Certa Pro Painters, Floor Coverings International, Stained Glass Overlay, Handyman Connection, Pillar to Post, BrandPoint Services and TLS. He has been involved in every aspect of the franchisor / franchisee relationship.

From growing brands domestically and internationally, mentoring franchise owners and working with individuals to understand if franchise ownership is the right step for them, Neonakis brings a wealth of experience to the table. Today, Neonakis uses his 20 years of experience in franchising, finance and business to help people realize their dream of independent business ownership. He currently lives in Shaker Heights, OH with his wife Stephanie and their children - Megan, Max and Alex. In his spare time, he enjoys remodeling houses, traveling and cooking.

SAGAR RAMBHIA

Sagar Rambhia is pursuing a dual degree B.A./M.D. at Case Western Reserve University and Case Western Reserve University School of Medicine through the Pre-Professional Scholars Program for Medicine. His academic interests lie in both Biochemistry and Economics.

Sagar's business interests include technological innovations and entrepreneurship. He has contributed to tech startups at the BIZDOM incubator in Cleveland, OH, StartX accelerator in Palo Alto, CA, and Y Combinator incubator in Mountain View, CA. Sagar Rambhia has won numerous accolades and awards associated with his science research endeavors by several prestigious organizations such as INTEL, the University of Chicago, and the Massachusetts Institute of Technology; including a minor planet in the main asteroid belt: 28505 Sagarrambhia (2000 CP83). Sagar also cofounded and led a nonprofit to provide computer refurbishing and repair. With the help of ~20 volunteers, they raised a fund for the Rotary Foundation - Gift of Life India project and opened a computer center for the School for Language and Communication Development in Long Island, NY.

He was raised in Muttontown, NY and currently resides in Cleveland, OH. He dedicates this book to his father, Dr. Hitendra Rambhia and mother, Priti Rambhia, along with his brother, Suraj and sister, Pooja.

ADITYA RENGASWAMY

Aditya Rengaswamy is currently pursuing a dual Masters / Bachelor's program in Accounting and is en-route to a Law Degree at Case Western Reserve University where he has been inducted to the prestigious Pre-Professional Scholars Program for Law.

Outside of academia, Aditya engages head and heart with various charitable works and entrepreneurial activity. While not working on his entrepreneurial ventures, his main interest is in charitable projects. He is the founder of the Cleveland Chapter of Kids Against Hunger and he has provided tens of thousands of meals for children since its founding. He is also the founder of Birthdays for the Blind, which has partnered with American Greetings to provide free audio-cards to the sight impaired for important celebrations in their lives. He is a life long entrepreneur whose main goal is to become a full time philanthropist if he is able to accumulate enough wealth to help tackle causes he believes in.

He was raised in Troy, MI and dedicates this book to his father and mother, Malini Rengaswamy and Rengaswamy Srinivasan, along with his brother Thejas.

Made in the USA
Middletown, DE
09 December 2015